THE MISEDUCATION OF THE FOREIGN REAL ESTATE INVESTOR

SHEMIKA JACKSON

THE MISEDUCATION OF THE FOREIGN REAL ESTATE INVESTOR

Navigating Urban Real Estate, Unveiling Deceptions, & Mastering the Art of U.S. Real Estate Investments

The Miseducation of the Foreign Real Estate Investor
Navigating Urban Real Estate, Unveiling Deceptions, & Mastering the Art of U.S. Real Estate Investments

Copyright © 2025 by **Shemika Jackson** All rights reserved.

No part of this publication may be reproduced, distributed, or transmitted in any form or by any means—including photocopying, recording, or other electronic or mechanical methods—without the prior written permission of the publisher, except in the case of brief quotations used in critical reviews and noncommercial uses permitted by copyright law.

This book is published by:
Meek Innovations, LLC

ISBN: 979-8-9991087-7-7

Disclaimer:
This publication is designed to provide general educational information about U.S. real estate investing for international investors. The author and publisher are not rendering legal, accounting, tax, financial, or investment advice. Laws and practices vary between cities, states, and countries, and they are subject to change. Readers are strongly encouraged to seek professional guidance from qualified attorneys, accountants, or investment advisors familiar with their specific circumstances before making any investment decisions.

The author has taken reasonable care in preparing this book and believes the information presented is accurate as of the date of publication. However, no warranties are made with respect to its accuracy or completeness, and the author and publisher disclaim any and all liability for damages resulting from the use of the material contained herein. Any examples, case studies, or references to specific individuals or companies are for illustrative purposes only and should not be considered endorsements or guarantees of any specific result.

Important Note: The author is a licensed real estate agent, but this book does not constitute a representation of any buyer or seller, nor does it create an agency relationship between the author and any reader. Any real estate transactions you pursue should be done in consultation with your own trusted professionals.

This book is not a substitute for legal due diligence, licensed financial planning, or business strategy consulting.

Use this information at your own risk.

Dedication

To my children —
Your laughter, strength, and brilliance remind me every day why I fight for legacy.
Everything I build is, so you never have to unlearn the lies I did.

To my family —
Thank you for being part of the soil that grew me.
Even the tough seasons gave me roots.

And to every foreign investor who's ever been lied to, misled, or left holding the bag —
This book is for you.
Not just so you can bounce back...
But so you can rise, rebuild, and own the game.

Table of Contents

Preface

Hey there, I'm Shemika aka *Meek the House Geek.*

I grew up in Cleveland, Ohio—inner-city born and raised. The same city where a lot of foreign investors love to invest. But what you see on paper rarely tells the full story of what's really happening in these neighborhoods.

I'm someone who's been through the trenches of real estate—licensed in two states, an active investor, and a trusted advisor to foreign investors looking to navigate the U.S. market. My journey isn't just about deals; it's about understanding the culture of the neighborhoods and the heartbeats of the communities where real estate lives.

I was raised on these same streets. I've walked these blocks, managed the properties, and closed on deals. I've seen the inside of courtrooms, boarded-up homes, and broken leases. I don't speak from theory—I speak from experience.

This book isn't about sugarcoating, hype, or big words to sound smart. It's about truth. The kind of truth I wish more people had before they spent their life savings on properties that were falling apart, in neighborhoods they didn't understand, sold to them by people who never had their best interests at heart. **They lacked what I now know are the fundamental pillars for success: clear strategy, structure, and consistent support.**

For years, I worked behind the scenes with international investors who bought properties in **urban inner-cities** like Cleveland, Detroit, Memphis, St. Louis, and Philly, to name a few. They came chasing opportunity, and instead found chaos: misinformation, lies, legal messes, properties they couldn't manage, tenants they couldn't control, and promises that turned into problems overnight.

Initially, I was simply closing deals and selling properties like any other agent or wholesaler. Then somehow, I became more of the boots on the ground. The one getting late-night calls and desperate emails. I'd walk into gutted properties—doors kicked in, windows boarded up, water damage from busted pipes—and listen to people pour out their stories through thick accents and broken trust.

"Shemika, please… I need help."
"Shemika, I didn't know this would happen."
"Shemika, I feel like a fool."

It wasn't a one-time thing. It happened almost every week for three years. And over time, it started to weigh on me. Because it wasn't just the real estate deals that were broken—it was the belief in the American dream and the sense of failure when that dream fell apart.

They weren't lacking intelligence.
They weren't greedy.
They were misled.
They were miseducated.

They were sold a version of real estate investing that sounded like a shortcut to freedom:

Buy a house in America.
Let someone else manage it.
Watch your money grow.

But the fine print was full of landmines.
They weren't told these homes were in war zones.
They weren't told tenants hadn't paid rent in months.
They weren't told about lead laws, eviction moratoriums, or how hard it is to rehab a house from across an ocean.

And they sure weren't taught how to verify the truth before sending their money.

I've seen smart people—doctors, engineers, business owners—fall for the same trap over and over again. They trusted the polished PowerPoints, the slick investor pitch decks, the websites that looked so official. But once the wire hit, the support vanished, the numbers didn't add up, and reality hit like a brick wall.
I know the streets because I lived them.
I know the system because I worked it.
I know the scams because I've spent years cleaning up the mess they leave behind.

This book is personal for me. It's been 18 months since I first wrote it and put it on the shelf—traumatized by the hell I went through and what I saw firsthand. I set myself on the sidelines, riding the bench. But the calls never stopped. Even now, 18 months later, those same clients keep calling for help—and here I am. As much as I wanted to ignore it, the inner pull from the Most High God has given me an assignment—one that I must obey. Because every time someone gets misled, it doesn't just hurt their bank account—it hurts entire communities. It deepens distrust. It damages neighborhoods. It turns potential partnerships into resentment. It makes everyone more guarded, more skeptical, and more isolated.

But it doesn't have to stay that way.

There's a better way to invest in U.S. real estate—one rooted in true education, **rock-solid strategy, structure, and unwavering support.** That's what this book is here to expose and rebuild. I want to tell the truth—not just the horror stories, but the hope too. Because I've seen investors do it the right way, leveraging **these very pillars** I'll show you. I've seen international buyers bring life back to abandoned blocks. I've seen legacy built, money protected, and purpose aligned.

This book is about unlearning the lies and learning the game.
It's about exposing what's broken and offering what's possible.

It's about making sure what happened to so many investors before you… never happens to you.
You don't have to be perfect.
You don't have to know everything.
But you do need to be ready.

If you've been burned, this is your redemption.
If you're just getting started, this is your warning.
And if you're ready to get real about investing in America the right way, this is your guide.

Let's rebuild what was stolen—starting with the truth.

Introduction

They sold you a dream. Now let's deal with the truth.

Let's be clear from the start:

If you're an international investor who's been burned investing in U.S. real estate, it's not because you're unqualified.
It's because you were miseducated.

You were targeted—on purpose.
You were sold a simplified dream that looked like freedom. Promised passive income, 20% returns, "fully managed" properties in "up-and-coming" neighborhoods. Told you could build wealth from overseas without ever setting foot on American soil. **What they didn't offer was the real strategy to navigate these markets, the proper structure to protect your assets, or the crucial support network to guide you.**

But here's what you weren't told:

- The "tenanted" house you bought was already in eviction court.
- The property manager wasn't even licensed.
- The numbers on the pitch deck didn't include taxes, vacancies, owner utilities, or repairs.
- The home had lead violations, back taxes, or major code issues.
- And the people who sold it to you? They disappeared the minute your wire cleared.

I wrote this book because the gap between what you were promised and what you actually bought is the same story I've seen too many times—and nobody's telling the truth about it.

Why This Keeps Happening

The U.S. real estate market—especially in distressed inner-city neighborhoods—has become a trap for international investors.

Why?
Because the numbers look good.
Because "cheap properties with high rent potential" are easy to sell.
Because people assume that anything in the U.S. must be regulated and safe.

But here's the real truth: inner-city investing in places like Cleveland, Detroit, Memphis, St. Louis or Baltimore is a different game.
It's not just numbers and contracts.
It's context. Culture. Street-by-street nuance.

And if you're not on the ground—or aligned with people who are—you're guessing.
And in real estate? **Guessing is expensive.**

But it's not just you.
The industry benefits from your lack of information.
There are entire businesses—wholesalers, fake investor groups, shady property managers, and online coaches—built on selling properties to people who don't know what to check, who to trust, or what questions to ask.

You're not just being sold property.
You're being sold a fantasy.
And fantasy has no warranty.

Who This Book Is For

This book is for the investor who's already made a move—and regrets it. For the one sitting on the sidelines but feeling pressure to jump in.

For the one who knows something doesn't feel right—but can't quite put their finger on what's off. And especially for the international investor who wants to build real wealth the right way—**with solid Strategy, protective Structure, and ongoing Support.**
If that's you? You're in the right place.

What This Book Will Do

This isn't a formula book.
It's not about spreadsheets or closing scripts.
It's about **re-education.**

I'm going to show you:

- What's really happening **behind the scenes** of these deals.
- When things tend to go wrong—and why you never saw it coming.
- Why the system is designed to keep you uninformed—and how to see through it.
- How your trust, silence, and distance make you the perfect target.
- And what it actually takes to win here—because yes, winning is still possible!

This isn't just about learning how to buy better.
This book is about unlearning the lies and learning the game.

It's about exposing what's broken and offering what's possible – **by showing you the foundational Strategy, Structure, and Support that true success demands.**

If You've Been Burned...

Let me say this:
You are not crazy.

You are not stupid.
And you are not alone.
You're part of a larger group of investors who were sold a dream and handed a disaster. But your story doesn't have to end there.

This book is your reset.
Your realignment.
Your release from the shame, confusion, or silence that came with being taken advantage of.

Let's tell the truth.
Let's expose the system.
Let's learn how to never let it happen again.

And then—when you're ready—
Let's rebuild what was stolen.

If You Haven't Been Burned—Yet...

Let me say this, too: Good.
But, you're not immune.
You're not above the hustle.
Even if you haven't been played, you're still vulnerable—because the game is designed to profit from your assumptions and your distance.
This book is your protection.
Your opportunity to unlearn what you've been told—and relearn what you really need to know. Because the real estate world doesn't care about your intentions—**it cares about your preparation**.

Don’t wait for a lesson that costs you everything.
Let this book be your shield—so you never have to write a chapter in your book titled “What I Didn’t Know.

Chapter 1: Welcome to the Inner-City

Beyond the Screen: Confronting the Unseen Realities of Urban Investment

The allure of a low price often blinds investors to the true cost of neglect.

I met an international investor who thought he'd found an easy win in Cleveland. He flew in from the UK—white sneakers fresh from the airport, spreadsheets and PDFs stacked in neat folders, but his eyes weren't wide with excitement. They were tight with frustration. He was already disappointed, and we hadn't even stepped into the city yet.

The story, as he later pieced it together for me on our ride from the airport, was an all too familiar one. He'd been browsing online forums, drawn in by the buzz of international real estate investment. A polished-looking website, stocked with photos of renovated homes and testimonials from seemingly ecstatic investors, had caught his eye. The company, with some generic name, promised 'turnkey' opportunities in 'emerging US markets.' Cleveland, they'd assured him, was ripe for the picking – low entry costs, high rental demand, and double-digit returns that made his pension fund look like a joke.

His initial contact was a smooth-talking representative, who sounded exactly like a man who knew how to close a deal. This guy sent him a glossy prospectus, filled with impressive-looking spreadsheets forecasting exponential growth. The duplex, identified only by its address and a blurry, slightly-too-good-to-be-true photo of a pristine facade, was presented as the 'deal of the year.' He assured him that the property had just undergone a 'light cosmetic renovation' and only needed a 'final polish' to be ready for tenants. The 'property manager' they recommended was presented as a local expert, deeply entrenched in the Cleveland market, with a proven track record of efficient, cost-effective turnovers. 'Just wire the funds, and we'll handle everything,' he had cooed over a grainy WhatsApp video call, 'You'll be cash-flowing in sixty days, tops.'

And he believed it. Why wouldn't he? He was a financial analyst by trade, accustomed to trusting data, projections, and professional assurances. The idea of passive income, a diversified portfolio, and escaping the dreary London drizzle for the promise of American opportunity was intoxicating. He'd wired over the purchase price – a substantial sum that represented a significant chunk of his savings – followed by the $14,000 for the 'rent-ready' work, all without a single flight, a single walk-through, or a single conversation with someone *on* the ground, in the actual neighborhood. He thought he was being smart, leveraging his capital from afar, trusting the experts. He'd bought into the dream, hook, line, and sinker, without ever dipping a toe into the water.

He'd bought this duplex sight unseen eight months earlier—no plan, no vision, just a promise someone sold him that he couldn't resist. He'd wired over the money, trusted the pitch, and paid his property manager $14,000 to "get it rent-ready." But here we were, months later, standing in front of a house that was still boarded up, still broken, and still bleeding him dry.

The hot water tanks and furnaces? Gone—stripped out and sold on the black market. The grass hadn't been cut once in eight months, turning the yard into a jungle of weeds and garbage. The porch sagged like it was tired of holding up the weight of his hopes. One window was boarded up; graffiti scrawled across the plywood: "NO TRESPASSING." The city had already sent violation notices, but the property manager had stopped answering the phone weeks ago.

He pulled out his phone, scrolling through WhatsApp messages from the property manager—screenshots of invoices, photos of supposed repairs that had never happened. His fingers tapped the screen again and again, trying to call. No answer. Just that hollow ringtone echoing in the sticky summer air.

"Fourteen thousand dollars," he muttered under his breath, not even looking at me. "I sent it all to him… he said the house would be ready in two months. He said it was easy money."

He looked up, his eyes meeting mine for the first time in a while. I could see it then—this wasn't a spreadsheet problem anymore. This was a man realizing he'd been lied to, face to face with a neighborhood he'd never known. He lacked the foundational **structure** that would have protected him, the clear **strategy** to navigate a volatile market, and the critical **support** network to catch him when he stumbled.

I let the silence stretch out between us. Sometimes that's the only way people start to hear the truth.

We stood there on a cracked sidewalk, looking at a house that had seen better days. His shoulders hunched as he took it all in—the peeling paint, the sagging roof, the boarded-up window. He tried to speak, but the words caught in his throat. The weight of the lies he'd been sold sat heavy on his chest, and I could feel it too.

A couple of kids were playing basketball in the street, using a milk crate nailed to a telephone pole as a hoop. Their laughter echoed down the block, a defiant soundtrack to the investor's disappointment. A woman in a headscarf swept her porch across the street, pausing every few minutes to glance over at us with wary eyes. An old man sat on his stoop, a can of cheap beer in his hand, watching us like he'd seen this movie play out a hundred times before.

The block has memory. It knows who comes here to build and who comes to take. And it was already sizing him up.

"This was going to change my life," he said finally, not with wonder but with cold certainty—like he was trying to convince himself it was still possible. Like he was already counting the rent checks in his head, even though there was no rent and no tenant in sight.

I wanted to laugh, not at him, but because I was utterly tired of seeing that familiar look: the investor enamored with the spreadsheet, yet completely blind to the realities of these type of investments. They didn't know the rules, so there was no way they'd know how to play.

Here's what he didn't see—what most of them never see:

These blocks aren't just lines on a map.
They're communities.
Generations of families have lived here—some for decades, some for lifetimes.
These houses aren't just doors or units or "cash-flowing assets."
They're legacies.
They're memories of grandparents who built them, of mothers who raised their children in them, of children who learned to ride bikes on these cracked sidewalks.

They're the living, breathing heart of a community that doesn't forget who treats it right—and who tries to take without giving back.

Look, I didn't grow up reading spreadsheets or making presentations about these neighborhoods. My mother was a homeowner, so we didn't rent a whole lot—she won a condemned duplex from a HUD lottery back in 1989 and did a complete rehab to make it livable for us. That was my first rehab, if you will.

I watched her fight the city inspectors, stretch every dollar, and turn that duplex into a home. We lived in the Buckeye-Shaker area back then, when it was still halfway decent. I remember telling people across town we lived in Shaker because we shared the same 44120 zip code, even though our block looked nothing like Shaker Heights.

It was survival pride, and everyone knew the difference anyway. I grew up around the stuff that happens in urban neighborhoods—the corner boys posted up near the store, the alleyways full of dumped furniture, the families who made a way out of nothing because no one else was coming to save them. I didn't know the first thing about landlording or investing back then, but I knew the culture. I knew the unspoken rules—who you could trust and who you couldn't. I knew the pride people took in surviving, even when the city forgot them.

The investor didn't see any of that. All he saw was a spreadsheet that said "18% ROI" and a promise of easy money. But this wasn't easy. This was Cleveland. This was a neighborhood that had been redlined and forgotten, where the city came around to ticket you for a missing gutter but never fixed the potholes in the middle of the street.

This was a neighborhood that knew how to survive—and how to spot a fake.

As we walked around the property, he kept talking about cutting costs—about the cheapest way to "make it rentable."

"I'll just patch the roof," he said, voice tight. "Paint the porch. Clean it up enough to get a tenant in."

I could hear the desperation in his tone. This wasn't about making it a home—it was about trying to save face, to salvage a bad bet. He didn't see the kids playing ball across the street. He didn't see the woman who'd lived on that porch for twenty years, sweeping away the dirt of the city like it was a daily ritual. He didn't see the old man who'd watched these houses change hands more times than he could count—watched investors come and go, promises made and broken.

"You see them?" I asked.

He glanced over, puzzled. "The kids? The woman? The old man?"

"Yeah," I said. "That's who you're really buying this house from. Not the bank, not the wholesaler. Them. They're the block. And they'll remember how you showed up." He frowned. "I'm not sure I follow."

"You don't have to yet," I said. "But you will." We kept walking. The sun was hot that day, the kind of heat that makes the asphalt shimmer like water. Sweat dripped down my neck. He kept talking numbers, but I was listening to the block. I gave a nod to the old man. He nodded back. That's how it is here—unspoken words, a silent test of respect.

Another Story, Another Lesson: The Illusion of Google Maps

The UK investor was far from an isolated incident. His story, and countless others like it, became the blueprint for the "miseducated investor" I'd encounter again and again. Each one believed they had found a shortcut, a loophole, a secret path to wealth, only to discover they'd walked straight into a minefield.

Take, for instance, the man from Israel. Let's call him Avi. Avi was a sharp, meticulous software engineer, the kind of person who built complex algorithms for a living. He approached everything with logic and data. When he decided to diversify his portfolio into U.S. real estate, he did what any modern, data-driven professional would do: he used Google Maps.

He'd spent weeks, he told me, meticulously "driving" through neighborhoods in Cleveland using Street View. He'd zoom in on properties, check out the surrounding blocks, look for signs of life, well-kept lawns, and decent-looking cars. He'd cross-reference with online property listings, comparing photos to what he saw on the digital street. He believed he was doing his due diligence. He was, in his mind, *seeing* the property.

He found a triplex that looked on Google Maps, perfectly acceptable. The street appeared quiet, tree-lined, with a few well-maintained homes nearby. The listing photos showed a freshly painted exterior and what looked like a decent interior. The numbers, presented by an online broker who specialized in "international investor deals," were fantastic: low purchase price, high projected rents, a clear path to passive income. It was exactly what he was looking for. He wired the money, confident in his remote investigation. He thought he had a solid **strategy** because he'd used the best tools available to him from overseas.

But Google Maps doesn't show you the water line in the basement.

It doesn't show you the community board meeting where residents are begging the city to address the rampant drug activity just two blocks over.

It doesn't show you the subtle, almost invisible, signs of neglect that only a local eye can spot—the specific type of graffiti that marks gang territory, the way certain vacant lots are used for illegal dumping, the quiet desperation in the eyes of a neighbor who's given up hope.

Avi discovered the truth when his **property manager** called, frantic, relaying the tenant's cries after a heavy rain: "The basement, it's a lake!" Avi tried to dismiss it as a fluke to the manager, thinking it was a one-off. But it wasn't. Every significant rainfall turned the triplex's basement into a swimming pool, rendering the lower unit uninhabitable and creating a breeding ground for mold. The previous owner, a flipper who knew exactly what he was doing, had simply painted over the water damage, knowing an international buyer wouldn't see it. Avi's lack of **structure** in his due diligence process — specifically, not having a trusted, independent inspection on the ground — left him completely exposed.

Then came the other relayed calls. Tenants complaining to the manager about strange cars idling at the corner, about late-night disturbances, about feeling unsafe. Avi, from thousands of miles away, tried to downplay these as isolated incidents, believing his manager would handle them. But the reality was, his "quiet, tree-lined street" was a stone's throw from a known high-crime area. The gang activity wasn't visible on Street View, but it was a lived reality for his tenants and the surrounding community. He had no support system on the ground to give him accurate, real-time intelligence about the block's true nature, and his property manager, chosen by the same online broker, was useless—either ignorant or complicit, simply collecting fees and ignoring the deeper issues.

Avi was an engineer. He understood systems. But he didn't understand the *human* system of the inner city. He didn't understand that Google Maps simply couldn't show him the **deep-seated history and true pulse of the neighborhood.** He lost half his life savings in six months, not because of a bad algorithm, but because he trusted pixels over people, data points over lived experience. He tried to apply a digital **strategy** to a profoundly analog reality.

His story was a stark reminder that even the most intelligent, data-driven individuals can fall prey to the illusion of remote investing if they don't have boots on the ground, a solid **structure** for vetting, and a reliable **support** network that understands the nuanced, often hidden, truths of these communities. He was trying to win a game he didn't understand, from a distance that made him blind.

The Turnkey Trap: When Pictures Lie

Another pattern I saw emerge with alarming frequency involved the allure of "turnkey" properties. The promise was irresistible: buy a fully renovated, tenant-occupied property that immediately generates cash flow, all managed by a professional company. It sounded like the ultimate passive investment, especially for someone thousands of miles away.

This was the trap that ensnared Sofia, a successful businesswoman from Chile. Sofia ran a thriving import-export company, accustomed to managing complex logistics and trusting reputable partners. When she decided to invest her hard-earned profits in U.S. real estate, she sought out what seemed like the safest, most hands-off option. She found a company online that boasted a portfolio of beautiful, supposedly cash-flowing properties in cities like Memphis. Their website was slick, their testimonials glowing, and their sales representative, a smooth talker, was incredibly reassuring.

He sent her a brochure filled with stunning, high-resolution photos of various properties. One, a charming three-bedroom house, caught her eye. The kitchen gleamed with new stainless-steel appliances, the bathrooms were spotless, and the living room looked freshly painted and staged. The numbers on the pro forma were equally impressive: a low purchase price, a signed lease with a long-term tenant, and a projected net operating income that promised a comfortable return. "It's completely hands-off, Sofia," he had promised over a video call, "We handle everything from acquisition to tenant placement to ongoing management. All you do is collect the rent."

Sofia, trusting the professionalism and the seemingly impeccable visuals, wired the money. She believed she had implemented a perfect **strategy** for passive income, relying on a company that promised to handle all the complexities. She thought she was building a secure **structure** for her investment by entrusting it to "experts."

But what Sofia didn't know was that the photos were staged. Not just "staged" with furniture but *staged* in a way that bordered on fraud. The gleaming kitchen was in a different house entirely. The freshly painted walls were only painted in the areas visible in the photos. The "long-term tenant" was a relative of the seller, placed there temporarily to make the property appear occupied and cash flowing. The reality was a house that had significant foundation issues, a leaky roof, and an electrical system that was barely up to code.

Sofia's first inkling of trouble came when she received a notice from the city of Memphis – a code violation for an unsafe porch. This was followed by **official correspondence from the city's housing department, relaying complaints from the actual tenant** about a lack of hot water and a persistent smell of mold. When Sofia tried to contact the company who sold her the property, the phone went straight to voicemail. Emails bounced back. The company's website, once so professional, suddenly seemed to have vanished.

She was left with a property she had never seen, thousands of miles away, that was quickly deteriorating and generating no income. The "professional management" had disappeared, leaving her to deal with city fines, disgruntled tenants, and a property that was now a liability, not an asset. Her lack of **support** – an independent, local representative to verify the property *before* purchase – had left her completely isolated when the scam unraveled. She had bought into a fantasy, a beautifully packaged lie, and the cost was not just her initial investment but the emotional burden of feeling utterly betrayed. The "turnkey" solution had turned into a financial and emotional nightmare, all because she relied on visual deception rather than verifiable truth and a robust **structure** for due diligence.

My Own Turnkey Trap: When Good Intentions Go Sideways

I've spent years cleaning up the messes left by these kinds of scams, helping investors navigate the wreckage of their miseducation. But the truth is, I also fell into my own version of the "turnkey trap"—not as a victim of fraud, but as someone trying to be the solution and people pleasing, only to discover how deeply woven the corruption was, and how easily even the best intentions can be compromised.

My journey into this specific kind of chaos began as an agent and wholesaler. I actually started wholesaling properties as a side hustle before the market crash in 2008 and then went all-in full-time in 2015. As a wholesaler, I was passionate about helping distressed sellers find quick, honest solutions, and I quickly became the go-to person in that area.

Being on the ground, I was seeing the properties firsthand and truly understanding the nuances of the blocks. I was the one who could tell the difference between a Google Maps illusion and the gritty reality. It was through this work that I met an Israeli investor—not Avi, but a different man whose properties, and those of his clients, had been thoroughly devastated by a contractor. His portfolio was a disaster, and he was desperate for someone he could trust to get things back on track.

I started volunteering to manage these rehab projects for investors. I'd go to their properties, acting as their boots on the ground, and quickly realized that often, no actual rehabs were taking place, despite invoices being paid. I saw the contractors' cutting corners, the property managers looking the other way, and the investors bleeding money from thousands of miles away. My Cleveland roots, my understanding of the culture, and my mother's lessons on stretching every dollar kicked in. I couldn't just stand by.

My goal was to genuinely help. I started overseeing the projects, making sure the work was actually getting done, and done right. Then, to avoid the houses sitting vacant and bleeding the investors dry with holding costs, I began placing tenants directly. I'd find good families, get them moved in, and then turn the property over to a traditional property management company.

This, however, did not sit well with the existing property management companies. They didn't like that I was cutting into their fees, or perhaps, exposing their inefficiencies. They didn't appreciate a local, knowledgeable person disrupting their comfortable, often shady, arrangements with remote investors. They made it difficult, creating friction and roadblocks.

So, in an effort to truly be a "one-stop shop" for these investors—to provide the seamless, honest service they desperately needed—I opened my own property management company. The vision was pure: to create a fully integrated solution, built on the principles of transparency and genuine care for both the property and the people. I wanted to make it great for the investor, to give them the peace of mind that came from having a single, trustworthy entity handling everything from acquisition to rehab to tenant placement and ongoing management.

But then, all hell broke loose.

I began taking on properties that I hadn't sold to these investors, properties that were already deep in disrepair, with existing problem tenants, and often, a history of neglect from previous managers. I was trying to be the hero, to fix every broken situation that came my way. But the scale of the corruption, the depth of the lies, and the sheer volume of problems I inherited quickly overwhelmed me.

I became exposed to the very corruption I was fighting against. I found myself making compromises, trying to uphold my commitment to manage properties that were fundamentally flawed, with tenants who had been mistreated, and in neighborhoods that were already battlegrounds. I was trying to put out fires that had been smoldering for years, often with limited resources and against a tide of systemic issues.

I lost myself. I lost my vision. The purity of my initial intention became muddied by the grim realities of the properties I was managing. I was knee-deep, woven into the very lies and broken systems I sought to dismantle. I was trying to fix everything for everyone, and in doing so, I began to compromise my own morals and integrity. The weight of upholding commitments on properties that were inherently problematic, sold by unscrupulous actors, became unbearable. I had to stop. I had to step back from the day-to-day management because I was becoming part of the problem, not the solution. I realized that even with the best intentions, without the right **strategy** for scaling, the proper **structure** to filter out bad deals, and the unwavering **support** of a truly aligned team, even *I* could get caught in the trap.

The Path Forward: Strategy, Structure, Support

The stories of the UK investor, Avi from Israel, and Sofia from Chile are not isolated incidents. They are patterns, repeated endlessly because the system is designed to exploit distance, trust, and a lack of on-the-ground knowledge. These investors, intelligent and well-meaning, fell victim to the same fundamental shortcomings: they lacked a clear **strategy**, a protective **structure**, and a reliable **support** system.

The UK investor, caught in a property manager's deceit, exemplified the critical absence of proper **structure**—no legal safeguards, no independent oversight, just blind faith. He also lacked the **support** to verify the work being done and the **strategy** to vet his partners effectively.

Avi, the engineer, believed his digital reconnaissance was a sound **strategy**, but it was built on incomplete data. He lacked the **support** of local eyes and ears to truly understand the neighborhood's context, and a robust **structure** for physical due diligence that would have revealed the hidden flaws.

Sofia, lured by the "turnkey" fantasy, put her trust in a company that offered neither true **strategy** nor genuine **support**. Her investment lacked the fundamental **structure** of independent verification and asset protection, leaving her exposed to outright fraud.

These aren't just cautionary tales; they are lessons in what *not* to do. They highlight the gaping holes in the typical international real estate investment journey. You can have all the capital in the world, all the ambition, and all the intelligence, but without these three pillars—**Strategy, Structure, and Support**—you are vulnerable.

This book is your re-education. It's designed to help you unlearn the dangerous assumptions that led these investors astray and to understand the real game.

In the coming chapters, we will break down each of these pillars, showing you not just what they are, but why they are absolutely non-negotiable for anyone serious about building sustainable wealth in U.S. real estate. We'll explore how to develop a winning **strategy** that fits your goals, how to build an ironclad **structure** to protect your assets, and how to cultivate the essential **support** network that will be your eyes, ears, and hands on the ground.

You've seen what happens when you don't have them.

Now, let's learn how to build them.

Chapter 2: The Awakening

A Mindset Shift for Real Investors

You can't win a game you don't understand...

Here's the truth:

Chapter one unveils a harsh truth: many foreign investors are deliberately **miseducated**, fed a steady diet of myths and half-truths designed to move properties, not empower them. They're lured by the promise of effortless, guaranteed passive income from afar, convinced the U.S. market is simple, that property managers handle everything, and that success is purely a matter of numbers on a spreadsheet.

But here's the truth they never heard: Real estate investing isn't passive, simple, or safe.

It's a business.
It's a system.
It's a responsibility.

And if you're not ready to treat it like that, you're not ready to play. This isn't a hobby; it's a serious venture that demands respect, diligence, and a fundamental shift in how you perceive "opportunity." The moment you decide to invest, you are stepping into a complex ecosystem with its own rules, its own history, and its own consequences for those who fail to understand it.

The Miseducation: Lies That Sold You Short

Let's call them out, these seductive lies that stripped so many investors of their money, their peace of mind, and their trust, leaving them chasing fantasies instead of building real wealth.

One of the most pervasive falsehoods is **"Numbers don't lie."** Oh, but they do—if you don't truly understand what they mean, what they omit, or how they've been manipulated. A spreadsheet is only as honest as its creator and the data points chosen for inclusion, or glaring exclusion. A projected 20% ROI is meaningless if it fails to account for a six-month vacancy, unexpected foundation repairs, or the spiraling costs of a protracted eviction. Numbers are merely tools, not prophets. They demand context, rigorous verification, and a healthy dose of skepticism. Without grasping the underlying realities of the market, the property, and the people involved, those impressive numbers are just a fantasy.

Perhaps the most dangerous deception is **"A manager is all you need."** While a property manager is an absolutely crucial part of your support system, they are never a substitute for your active involvement and understanding. They are an extension of your business, not the business itself. You must know how to vet them, how to hold them accountable, and how to identify critical red flags, like when communication mysteriously goes silent or reports become vaguely insufficient. If you cannot effectively oversee your manager, you simply cannot manage your property. The UK investor learned this harsh lesson when his manager vanished, leaving him with a gutted house and a $14,000 hole in his pocket. He had mistakenly assumed the manager was *the* solution, rather than *a responsibility* he needed to manage.

Then there's the alluring promise of **"It's passive income."** The dream of money flowing into your bank account while you sleep, without lifting a finger, is the ultimate seduction. Yet, real estate, particularly in inner-city markets, is rarely truly passive. It demands active management, even when you delegate tasks. It involves dealing with a leaky roof in the middle of the night, mediating tenant disputes, navigating city code violations, or fighting for months in eviction court when a tenant stops paying. True passive income is the *result* of a well-executed strategy, a solid structure, and reliable support—it is not the starting point. It requires significant upfront work, ongoing vigilance, and the readiness to step in when things inevitably go sideways.

Finally, the broad assertion **"If you buy in America, you're set"** is a profound act of miseducation. The U.S. market is vast and incredibly diverse. Acquiring a property in a stable, affluent suburban neighborhood is fundamentally different from buying a distressed duplex in a redlined inner-city community. The former might offer relative stability; the latter is a battleground. Assuming all of America is the same, or that "cheap" automatically equates to "opportunity," is a dangerous fallacy. You might unwittingly buy into a war zone you've never seen, a community grappling with decades of systemic neglect, where the rules of engagement are entirely different from what you're accustomed to.

They didn't teach you about:

- **How to analyze what kind of investor you *actually* are.** Your unique personality, your financial capacity, and your true risk tolerance should be the driving force behind your strategy, not someone else's hype. Are you genuinely comfortable with the volatility and rapid pace of flipping, or is the steady, slower growth of long-term rentals a more suitable fit for your temperament? Do you possess the emotional bandwidth to deal with tenant issues, or do you require an exceptionally robust management system? Your internal compass must always guide your external actions.

- **Why every number on the spreadsheet needs real-world context.** Cash flow projections become useless if you lack understanding of the specific neighborhood, the prevailing market cycles, the true physical condition of the property, and all realistic exit options. Avi, the engineer, discovered this when Google Maps failed to reveal the water in the basement or the gang activity down the street. The numbers are merely a starting point, never the complete story. They absolutely must be validated by boots-on-the-ground intelligence and a deep understanding of the local ecosystem.
- **How to build a real exit strategy *before* you ever wire a single dollar.** The adage rings true: you make your money when you buy, not when you sell. A property is not a genuine investment until you have a clear plan for how you're going to get your capital back, ideally with a profit. What if the market shifts unexpectedly? What if the tenant never pays? What if the rehabilitation costs spiral wildly out of control? A sound strategy always includes a clear Plan A, Plan B, and even a "Plan C" for safely exiting, minimizing potential losses, and rigorously protecting your capital. Without a robust exit strategy, you're not truly investing; you're simply buying a problem.

The Real Awakening: A Call That Changed Everything

After that initial, eye-opening trip to Cleveland, the investor from the UK flew home. He was still hopeful, but clearly shaken by what he'd seen. He sent me a polite, though somewhat guarded, thank-you message. I sensed he'd heard me, but I wasn't entirely convinced he was ready to truly listen, to fully absorb the hard truths I'd laid out. He still seemed to cling to the spreadsheet dream, hoping to salvage it.

A week later, he called me again.

His voice was distinctly different—quieter, more deliberate, stripped of the initial frustration and replaced with a sobering, profound realization. He was no longer looking for quick fixes. He was searching for genuine understanding.

"Shemika," he began, his voice now calm, "I've been thinking a lot about what you said. At first, I honestly thought you were trying to scare me off, trying to discourage me from investing in America. I thought you were just being negative. But now I see you were trying to protect me. I understand now that what I saw on paper was not the full reality. I'm going to take my time and build it right. No shortcuts. I need to understand the game before I try to play it."

Even over the phone, across thousands of miles, I could feel the profound shift in him. It wasn't merely a change of mind; it was a fundamental reorientation of his entire mindset. He had transitioned from blindly chasing a fantasy to bravely embracing a difficult, essential truth.

That moment marked a true awakening—not just for him, but for me too. Because it vividly reminded me why I do this work:

I don't sell dreams. I share the truth—even when it's not what people initially want to hear. I don't promise easy money; I promise real education. I don't offer shortcuts; I offer a clear roadmap to sustainable success.

My Partner's Comment: *"Are You Trying to Talk Him Out of It?"*

I remember later that week, my partner at the time—someone more accustomed to the traditional, often aggressive, sales-driven side of real estate—pulled me aside. He had overheard parts of my conversation with the UK investor.

With a hint of concern, and perhaps a touch of exasperation, he said, "You know, Meek, it sounded like you were trying to talk that investor out of buying here. We need to close deals, not scare people off."

I chuckled softly, a knowing, weary laugh, and replied, "No, I'm trying to talk him out of buying in blind. I'm trying to talk him into building something real, not just buying a problem."

Because here's the fundamental truth:

I'm not here to sugarcoat the reality of the market. I'm here to show its raw, complex beauty alongside its inherent challenges. I'm not here to hype a deal I wouldn't personally touch. My integrity is absolutely non-negotiable. I'm here to guide investors on how to see the whole picture—the good and the bad—so they can make a genuinely informed decision, rather than simply chasing a spreadsheet's promise. This demands understanding the risks just as clearly as the rewards, and being prepared for both.

Some people believe that telling the unvarnished truth about difficulties is discouraging, that it will simply make people walk away. But I firmly believe that's the *only* way to truly play this game, especially for the long term. It's the only way to attract the right kind of investor—the one who is serious, resilient, and deeply committed to building something sustainable, not just making a quick buck. Those who are ready for the truth are precisely the ones who will ultimately succeed.

The Truth: Strategy is the Antidote to Miseducation

The core of this crucial mindset shift lies in understanding and embracing a true **strategy**. It is the first pillar, the guiding force that dictates every single decision you make. Without a clear, well-defined strategy, you are merely reacting to fleeting opportunities, chasing shiny objects, and operating on hopeful wishes rather than a meticulously designed plan.

Because here's the real play:

Strategy is how you move past the pervasive myths. It's how you stop chasing what *sounds* good and start building what *actually works.* Your strategy is the personalized blueprint for your entire investment journey, meticulously tailored to your specific goals, your unique risk tolerance, and your available resources. It is emphatically not a one-size-fits-all solution; it is a deeply personal and thoroughly researched roadmap.

Strategy means:

- **Picking the right markets**, and not just settling for what's cheap. This extends far beyond mere zip codes to a deep understanding of specific micro-markets, their unique community dynamics, and the true trajectory of a particular block. It means keenly discerning why one street might consistently thrive while another, just a few blocks away, struggles. It's about differentiating genuine opportunity from superficial appearance.
- **Choosing the right investment model**, rather than simply following the latest hype. Are you a long-term holder primarily focused on consistent cash flow and gradual appreciation, or a short-term flipper seeking quick capital gains? Each distinct approach demands a different methodology for property

selection, renovation execution, and exit planning. Your strategy must be in authentic alignment with your financial aspirations and your capacity for active involvement.

- **Learning how to vet deals**, instead of simply trusting persuasive pitches. This is where the rubber meets the road, demanding forensic due diligence. This includes independent inspections, meticulous title searches, rigorous verification of tenant histories, and the painstaking scrutiny of every single number presented. It means proceeding with the assumption that every pitch conceals hidden liabilities until proven otherwise. Your comprehensive strategy must incorporate a rigorous vetting process explicitly designed to protect your hard-earned capital.
- **Knowing your numbers**, and not just believing compelling PowerPoint slides. This isn't merely about the purchase price and projected rent. It's about comprehending *all* the costs involved: acquisition fees, closing costs, realistic rehabilitation budgets (always with contingencies), ongoing operating expenses, property taxes, insurance premiums, and realistic vacancy rates. It's about meticulously building your *own* pro forma, stress-testing it against various scenarios, and truly understanding the actual, sustainable cash flow.
- **Having a clear exit plan before you ever wire the money.** What if your primary strategy doesn't unfold as anticipated? Do you possess a clear, predefined path to sell, refinance, or pivot your approach? An exit strategy is emphatically not a sign of weakness; it is, in fact, the hallmark of a robust, resilient investment plan. It’s fundamentally about protecting your downside and ensuring you are never forced into a desperate, value-eroding sale.

When you are crystal clear on your strategy, you are no longer passively chasing deals—you are actively building a sturdy foundation. You are no longer guessing—you are leading. And that is precisely what separates truly successful investors from the rest. It's the profound difference between being a pawn in someone else's game and being the masterful player who understands every move.

Let Me Tell You About David

I had a client from the Netherlands—let's call him David. He was sharp, determined, and genuinely ready to build something real for his family. He had a successful career, a comfortable life, and a strong, admirable desire to create generational wealth through real estate.

David wasn't new to investing in general—he was just new to investing in the U.S. He had consumed all the online videos, absorbed all the hype, and, unfortunately, bought into the pervasive myth that "if you buy a property in America, you're already winning." He viewed the relatively low property prices in certain U.S. cities as an undeniable opportunity; a simple arbitrage play that, to him, couldn't possibly go wrong.

So, with this incomplete understanding, he wired money for a duplex in a city he'd never personally visited, relying solely on a broker he'd only ever spoken to online. He bought it fully tenanted, or so he was told. There was no real plan beyond the simple directive of "buy it, collect rent." No robust systems for oversight were in place, no clear understanding of the local market's unique challenges, and certainly no thought had been given to an exit strategy if things were to go sideways. He fundamentally believed that the simple act of buying was the strategy itself.

Six months later, he called me—his voice now tinged with panic, a stark contrast to his initial confident demeanor. He reported that the tenants hadn't paid rent in three months, and the "property manager" had vanished—no answers, no updates, just a silent phone line. The city was now hitting him with fines for violations he didn't even know about, for issues that clearly predated his ownership. The property, once optimistically described as "turnkey," was now visibly deteriorating, showing clear signs of neglect that would have been immediately obvious to anyone physically on the ground.

I asked him, gently, trying to guide him to the root of the problem: "David, what was your plan when you bought it? What was your strategy for dealing with non-paying tenants, or a disappearing manager, or unexpected city fines?"

Silence. A long, heavy silence stretched across the thousands of miles between us.

Then he spoke, his voice barely a whisper, "I guess I just wanted to prove I could do it. I didn't think about how to keep it going. I thought buying was the hard part. I didn't have a plan for after the purchase."

David's story perfectly illustrates why this mindset shift is so profoundly important. He wasn't a bad investor. He wasn't unintelligent or lazy. He was simply focused entirely on the acquisition—without knowing how to build, how to protect, or how to sustain his investment. He didn't know his non-negotiables. He didn't know how to vet his team for true accountability. He didn't know what success truly looked like for him beyond the initial acquisition. His strategy was critically incomplete, a half-baked idea based on dangerous assumptions, not on reality.

What Kind of Investor Do You Want to Be?

That's the first real question that truly matters, and it's a question of mindset that must definitively precede any discussion of properties or profits. Because there's a profound difference between merely being a buyer and being a true investor. A buyer gets excited about the deal. They chase the next shiny object, the lowest price, the highest projected return, and their primary focus is on acquisition. An investor, however, remains disciplined, focused on the long game. They understand that the deal is just one intricate piece of a much larger puzzle, and their core focus is on building, protecting, and sustaining wealth over time.

A buyer just wants in, eager to participate, often without fully understanding the underlying rules or inherent risks. An investor, on the other hand, knows precisely how to stay in the game—and crucially, how to get out if circumstances change. They anticipate challenges, meticulously build contingencies, and consistently prioritize capital preservation over speculative gains.

The truth is: You're not just here to own a property—you're here to build something. You're here to create a lasting legacy, to secure your financial future, or to achieve a specific personal goal. This requires a conscious, deliberate decision about your fundamental investment identity.

That means knowing your style. Are you here to hold properties long-term for consistent cash flow, to flip them short-term for quick capital gains, or to explore more creative strategies like seller financing or lease options? Each distinct style demands a different approach to property selection, risk management, and time commitment. Your strategy must be an authentic reflection of who you are and what you're genuinely capable of.

It also means understanding your true risk tolerance. How much stress can you genuinely handle? Are you comfortable with the potential for significant, unexpected repairs, ongoing tenant issues, or volatile market fluctuations? Be brutally honest with yourself. If the mere thought of a major unexpected expense keeps you awake at night, then your strategy unequivocally needs to be more conservative, focusing on lower-risk properties and building exceptionally robust reserves.

Finally, you must set boundaries on what you will and won't touch. This is about clearly defining your investment perimeter. What specific property conditions are absolute non-starters? What neighborhoods are simply too risky for your comfort level? What kind of partners will you absolutely avoid, regardless of the perceived opportunity? These boundaries are not limitations; they are indispensable guardrails that protect both your capital and your peace of mind.

Because until you know what kind of investor you truly want to be, you're essentially just guessing—signing checks without a real, coherent plan, and susceptible to every smooth-talking salesperson who promises you the moon.

What Are Your Non-Negotiables?

The miseducation told you: Be flexible. Just get in. Worry about the details later. This is the dangerous mantra of the desperate, the naive, and the soon-to-be burned. It's the direct path to compromise, regret, and ultimately, financial ruin.

That's how you end up in court, burdened with unexpected liens, or saddled with tenants who mysteriously stop paying the very day after you close the deal. That's precisely how you inherit someone else's problem and tragically make it your very own.

The truth? You need hard lines in the sand. You need non-negotiables.

These are the fundamental standards you simply won't compromise on—no matter how enticing the numbers might appear, no matter how persuasive the sales pitch. These are your personal and financial red lines, the absolute minimum standards you demand from your investments, from your partners, and, critically, from yourself.

For example, you might declare, "I won't buy in a zip code I haven't thoroughly researched myself, extending far beyond just online data. This means understanding the block-by-block reality, the intricate community dynamics, and the true trajectory of the area." Another non-negotiable could be, "I won't work with a property manager I haven't independently vetted, complete with multiple reference checks and a clear, pre-established communication plan. Their license, their professional reputation, and their unwavering accountability are paramount." Perhaps, "I won't buy a property if I can't clearly envision a realistic exit plan, including robust contingencies for unforeseen circumstances. This means knowing precisely how you'll retrieve your capital, even if the primary plan fails to materialize." Or, "I won't blindly trust a pro forma that hasn't been rigorously stress-tested with conservative, realistic vacancy rates and ample repair reserves. I will meticulously build and verify my own numbers." And finally, "I won't rely on photos alone; I will demand independent inspections and local, on-the-ground verification for every property I consider seriously."

Non-negotiables aren't about saying "no" to opportunity—they are, in fact, about powerfully saying "yes" to only the right opportunities. They effectively filter out the noise, protect you from impulsive decisions, and ensure that every single investment aligns precisely with your defined strategy and your true risk tolerance. They are the undeniable bedrock of a disciplined, successful investor mindset.

What Does Success Actually Look Like for You—And *Why*?

The miseducation told you: "How many doors do you own?" "How big is your ROI?" "How fast can you close?" They made you believe that success was solely about the numbers—bragging rights, not actual, meaningful results. They fed you a superficial definition of success meticulously designed to keep you endlessly chasing the next deal, rather than building something truly meaningful and sustainable for your life.

But real success is deeply personal. It's about what's sustainable. What's safe. What genuinely allows you to sleep peacefully at night. It's about meticulously aligning your investments with your overarching life goals, not merely chasing arbitrary metrics defined by others.

For you, success might be having two solid properties that reliably generate cash flow—because you're committed to playing the long game, prioritizing consistent, predictable income that meaningfully contributes to your financial freedom, without the constant stress of chasing endless deals or managing crises. It could be building enough truly passive income to fully pay for your child's college education—because that's what genuinely matters most to you. In this context, success becomes a tangible, life-changing impact on your family's future, a specific financial milestone achieved through diligent, strategic investing. Perhaps success is creating real partnerships that genuinely help put people in homes they are proud to live in—because that's how you define impact and lasting legacy. This shifts the focus from purely transactional gains to a more holistic view of wealth, where your investments actively contribute positively to the community and imbue your efforts with a profound sense of purpose. It might also be achieving a certain, deeply satisfying level of peace of mind, knowing your assets are thoroughly protected and your team is unfailingly reliable, allowing you to focus on other, equally important aspects of your life. Or success could mean building a truly diversified portfolio that effectively mitigates risk and provides unwavering stability, rather than foolishly putting all your hard-earned eggs in one speculative basket.

Until you define what success truly means for you, you're merely chasing someone else's definition, someone else's dream, and most likely, inadvertently repeating someone else's mistakes.

Let's Wrap This Up

So let me ask you again—pause, breathe deeply, and write this down if you need to. Be brutally honest with yourself. This moment of clarity is the foundational step of your awakening:

- What kind of investor do you want to be? Are you a Buyer or a true Investor? Do you lean towards Flipper or Long-Term Holder? Do you seek genuinely Passive income or are you ready for Active involvement?
- What are your non-negotiables? Define the hard lines you will not cross, the absolute standards you will never compromise on.
- What does success look like for you—and why? Beyond the mere numbers, what is the profound, real impact you desire on your life and your lasting legacy?

Because once you definitively know these things? You're no longer guessing. You're leading. You're investing like someone who's in this for the long haul—not just chasing fleeting headlines. You're building a sustainable business, not just haphazardly buying a house. You're becoming the undeniable master of your own investment journey, rather than a mere pawn in someone else's game.

Alright—now that you have clarity on what kind of investor you are, what your non-negotiables truly are, and what real success looks like for you…

We can now begin building a robust strategy that perfectly fits you—not some generic sales pitch. A strategy that is deeply rooted in who you are and what you genuinely want—so you're not just chasing deals. You're actively building a legacy.

Reflection Check-In:

- What have I been taught to chase—and what's actually worth chasing for me, personally?
- Where do I need to pause and rethink what I'm willing to accept—and what I'm not?
- How can I begin investing like an investor, and not just a buyer?

Let's get you ready for the real game. Chapter 3 is where we start laying the critical foundation, diving into the essential pillar of Structure.

Chapter 3: Strategy

Crafting Your Personalized Blueprint

The spreadsheet shows you numbers. Your strategy defines your future. Build accordingly.

In "The Awakening," we fundamentally shifted your mindset. You began to see real estate not as a passive investment, but as a dynamic business demanding your informed participation.

You started to ask the crucial questions:

What kind of investor do I want to be?
What are my non-negotiables?
What does success truly look like for me?

These were the first brushstrokes on your personal canvas, moving you away from the miseducation and towards a path of clarity.

Now, we move from the conceptual to the concrete. This chapter is about systematically unpacking **Strategy**—the personalized roadmap that will dictate ***what*** you invest in, ***where*** you invest, ***how*** you approach every aspect of the deal, and crucially, *why* you are making these specific choices.

Without a meticulously crafted, deeply understood strategy, even the most promising property can quickly become a source of confusion, frustration, and significant financial loss. This is your blueprint, designed not by a salesperson or a hyped webinar, but by you, for you, based on your unique circumstances and aspirations. It is the intellectual backbone of your entire investment operation.

Beyond the Hype: Defining Your "Why" and "What" with Precision

Before you even glance at a property listing, before you calculate a single ROI, you must first define your core purpose. The miseducation often skips this crucial, introspective step, pushing you directly to properties that fit a seller's agenda, not your own. They want you to buy *their* deal, not *your* ideal investment. But a real strategy, one that leads to sustainable success and peace of mind, begins with deep introspection and honest self-assessment.

Revisit Your Investor Identity with Granular Detail: Who Are You, *Really*?

In Chapter 2, we touched on this, but let's dig deeper. Your **investor identity** isn't just a label you pick; it's a reflection of your inherent personality, your current financial bandwidth, your true psychological risk tolerance, and your genuine capacity for time commitment. Ignoring these internal factors is a recipe for misalignment and stress.

First, let's get precise about your **financial goals**. Are you chasing aggressive capital appreciation—often high-risk, high reward, demanding more active management and market timing? Do you prioritize consistent monthly cash flow—more stable, long-term, and less prone to market fluctuations? Or are you seeking a strategic blend of both? Be specific with numbers and timelines. For instance, you might declare, "I need to generate $2,000 USD in net cash flow per month within 24 months to supplement my pension," or "I aim for a 20% annualized return on equity over 5 years through property appreciation and strategic refinancing." Whether you need to replace an existing income or simply supplement it, your goals will ultimately dictate the types of properties, markets, and investment models you should pursue.

Next, consider your **true psychological risk tolerance**. This goes beyond mere numbers on a page. Are you genuinely comfortable with the potential for significant property damage, like a burst pipe causing extensive flooding, or difficult tenants requiring eviction proceedings? Can you handle major market fluctuations, such as property values dropping or interest rates rising? Or do you inherently prefer lower-risk, more predictable investments, even if the returns are more modest? Your personality type—whether you're highly analytical and risk-averse, or adventurous and comfortable with uncertainty—should profoundly inform this. An investor who fears volatility, for example, should not pursue high-leverage flips in emerging markets.

Be honest about **how much time you can realistically commit to oversight**. Even with the best property manager, overseas investing requires active involvement. Are you prepared for weekly check-ins, monthly financial reviews, quarterly property inspections (via your local support), and occasional urgent problem-solving, such as coordinating a major repair or dealing with a legal notice? Or do your current professional and personal commitments demand an even more hands-off approach? This might necessitate a different type of asset, such as a triple-net lease commercial property, or a more robust, truly full-service management structure, which naturally comes at a higher cost.

Consider your **current real estate experience level**. Are you a seasoned businessperson translating transferable skills to real estate, or are you a complete novice with no prior property management or investment experience? Your experience level directly influences the complexity and risk profile of deals you should realistically consider. A novice should start with simpler, lower-risk properties and build experience before tackling complex rehabs or multi-family units.

Finally, clarify your **personal values and ethical considerations**. Do you want your investments to contribute positively to community revitalization, or provide safe and affordable housing? Or are you solely focused on maximizing profit, regardless of social impact? Aligning your investments with your values can lead to greater personal fulfillment, a stronger sense of purpose, and often, more sustainable success, as ethical practices tend to build goodwill and reduce long-term problems. An investor committed to community uplift, for instance, might focus on properties that can be genuinely improved and rented to stable families, rather than quick, superficial flips.

Active vs. Passive: Understanding Your True Level of Engagement

Many international investors are sold on the dream of "passive income" in real estate. While real estate can certainly provide consistent cash flow, true, zero-effort passivity is a myth, especially when operating from afar in dynamic markets. Even with the best property manager, you are still the CEO of your investment business, responsible for strategic direction and oversight.

"Passive" Oversight describes the CEO role. This level of engagement means you set the overarching strategy, meticulously review all incoming reports—financial, maintenance, and tenant updates—approve major expenditures, and hold your Support System accountable to predefined Key Performance Indicators (KPIs). This still requires significant time, focus, and a deep understanding of your business's operations. You aren't physically working on the property, but you are actively managing the managers.

"Active" Engagement, on the other hand, means you're a more hands-on CEO. This might involve more frequent, in-depth communication with your team, deeper personal involvement in renovation decisions—such as selecting materials or reviewing detailed plans—or even pursuing more complex deals like commercial properties, ground-up development projects, or short-term rentals that demand constant attention. This level requires more time, specialized knowledge, and a willingness to be deeply involved in the operational minutiae.

Defining your desired level of engagement upfront is crucial. This helps you choose the right property types, the most suitable markets, and, crucially, the right Support System that can genuinely meet your needs and expectations without leading to burnout or neglect. Misalignment here is a common source of investor frustration.

The Power of Precision: Micro-Market Selection – Beyond the City Name

The single biggest, and arguably most costly, mistake many miseducated investors make is buying a property in a "city" without understanding the **specific neighborhood or even block** where it's located. A city like Cleveland, Detroit, Memphis, or Baltimore isn't a uniform whole; it's a complex tapestry, a patchwork of dozens, if not hundreds, of distinct micro-markets. Each micro-market possesses its own unique dynamics, specific challenges, and hidden opportunities. Buying a property in a "good neighborhood" in one part of the city can be wildly different, in terms of risk and return, from buying an identical property just a few streets away in another micro-market.

Why "City" Is Too Broad: The Block-by-Block Reality is Everything

Hyper-local dynamics are determinative. Factors such as crime rates—even within the same zip code—school quality, which can change dramatically across a few blocks, access to essential amenities like a walk to a grocery store versus a 30-minute bus ride, presence of public transit, availability of parks and green spaces, owner-occupancy rates—a key indicator of neighborhood stability—and the presence of active community initiatives can vary dramatically from one block to the next. These are the intangible forces that shape a neighborhood's desirability and future.

Property value fluctuations are granular. An identical house might be worth 50% more or less just a few streets away due to these hyper-local factors. A property on a block with well-maintained homes and engaged residents will command higher rents and appreciate faster than an identical property on a block riddled with blight and vacancy, even if they share the same zip code.

Lastly, **tenant pools are specific to the block**. Different micro-markets naturally attract different tenant demographics. A block near a university might attract students, while one near a hospital might attract medical professionals, and another in a struggling area might attract Section 8 tenants. Understanding these specific tenant pools directly impacts your realistic rent levels, expected vacancy rates, and the overall quality and stability of your tenancy.

Key Factors to Research for Precise Micro-Market Selection

When researching a micro-market, delve into the **demographics**: Who lives here, and are they your ideal tenant? Go beyond broad census data to research income levels, average household sizes, age ranges, and predominant employment types in that specific area. Ensure these demographics align with your target tenant profile. For instance, if you're targeting young professionals, you need to be in an area with a growing job market and amenities that appeal to them.

Identify the **economic drivers** that fuel this specific local economy. Look for major employers like universities, hospitals, large corporations, or tech hubs, as well as new commercial developments or significant government investments like new public transit lines or community centers. Is the local job market stable, growing, or declining? A diverse and growing economic base provides stability for your tenant pool.

Don't rely on anecdotes for **crime rates**; seek data. Check official local police department statistics mapped by precinct or specific neighborhood. Understand the types of crime prevalent, whether property crime or violent crime, and analyze trends over time—are rates increasing or decreasing? This directly impacts tenant safety and desirability.

School districts are often an indicator of stability. Even if you're not targeting families with children, good school districts often correlate strongly with stable, owner-occupied neighborhoods, higher property values, and a more desirable area for tenants and future buyers. Research specific school ratings and trends.

Consider the **infrastructure and amenities** that shape daily life. Proximity to essential infrastructure—reliable utilities, well-maintained roads—and amenities—public transportation routes, major highways, grocery stores, hospitals, parks, cultural attractions, entertainment districts—can significantly impact a property's desirability, rental rates, and future appreciation. Convenience is a powerful driver for tenants.

Analyze **population trends**: Is the area growing or shrinking? Is the population stable, growing, or declining in that specific micro-area?

Are young professionals or families moving in, or is it an aging population with outward migration? Population growth, especially of your target demographic, is a positive indicator.

Look for **blight and vacancy rates** as visual cues and data points. Drive, or have your local Support System drive and film, through the area at different times of day. Are there many boarded-up homes or vacant, unkempt lots? High vacancy rates in the immediate vicinity can depress rents, increase crime, and signal a declining area, significantly increasing your risk.

Finally, assess **community initiatives and leadership**. Are there active neighborhood associations, Community Development Corporations (CDCs), or local non-profits working to improve the area? Is there visible community leadership and engagement? This indicates local pride, collective action, and potential for positive, sustainable change, which can significantly enhance your investment's long-term prospects.

Essential Tools for Micro-Market Research (From Afar)

Leverage technology for your research but always cross-reference and verify with human intelligence. **City Planning and Development Websites** for most major U.S. cities and counties offer robust planning department websites with publicly accessible zoning maps, detailed demographic data, comprehensive plans for future development, and records of recent permits issued. These are goldmines of information.

Local News Archives & Community Blogs found via Google provide invaluable qualitative insights into neighborhood issues, successes, local politics, and general sentiment that official data might miss. Look for recurring themes or persistent problems. **Police Department Websites** offer access to official crime statistics mapped by precinct or specific neighborhood, with some departments even having interactive crime maps.

Economic Development Agencies, whether government or non-profit, often publish reports on job growth, industry trends, major corporate investments, and new infrastructure projects in the area. The **U.S. Census Data** provides incredibly detailed demographic and economic data down to the block group level, allowing for granular analysis of income, education, housing types, and population changes.

While not real-time, **Google Street View & Google Earth** can give you a visual sense of the neighborhood's condition, surrounding properties, and amenities. Use them as a first pass to filter out obvious non-starters, but always verify with your local Support System for current conditions. **Local Real Estate Associations & MLS Data** often publish market reports and can connect you with knowledgeable local agents who have access to Multiple Listing Service (MLS) data for detailed property and rental comparisons. Finally, **Online Rental Platforms** like Zillow and Apartments.com are excellent for researching current rental listings and recently rented properties in your target micro-market to get a realistic sense of achievable rent prices.

The goal is to understand the soul of the neighborhood, its current pulse, and its likely trajectory. This foundational, hyper-local knowledge allows you to select markets that truly align with your strategy and risk tolerance, moving far beyond the superficial numbers presented by eager sellers and into the realm of informed, strategic decision-making.

Choosing Your Investment Model: Alignment with Your Strategy

Once you've identified your ideal micro-market, your overarching strategy dictates the specific investment model you'll pursue. Each model has distinct characteristics, risk profiles, operational requirements, and financial implications. Misaligning your model with your resources and goals is a common strategic error.

1. Buy-and-Hold (The Long Game: Cash Flow and Steady Appreciation Focus)

This model involves acquiring properties, renting them out, and holding them for the long term, typically five or more years, to generate consistent monthly rental income (cash flow) and benefit from gradual property appreciation.

Strategic Considerations for Buy-and-Hold: Focus on "rent-ready" properties or those needing only light, cosmetic rehab to minimize immediate capital expenditure (CapEx) and accelerate tenant placement and cash flow. **Stable, long-term tenants** are key, so target working-class families, young professionals, or those supported by robust programs like Section 8. Rigorous tenant screening is paramount.

When evaluating financially, focus on **Cash-on-Cash Return (CoC)**, which is your annual pre-tax cash flow divided by total cash invested, measuring the percentage return on your actual cash outlay. Also consider the **Capitalization Rate (Cap Rate)**, which is Net Operating Income (NOI) divided by the property's purchase price, offering a quick snapshot of profitability for an all-cash purchase.

Crucial for longevity are **essential reserves**. Always budget for vacancies, perhaps 5-10% of gross rent annually, and Capital Expenditures (CapEx) for major components like roofs, HVAC, or foundations, often 10-15% of gross rent annually for older properties. Don't forget a general contingency fund for unexpected repairs.

The **pros** of buy-and-hold include stable, predictable income, building long-term equity, benefiting from inflation, less susceptibility to short-term market fluctuations, and potential tax benefits through depreciation. The **cons** are slower capital growth, ongoing management requirements, an illiquid asset, and the potential for unexpected major repairs to impact cash flow if reserves are insufficient.

2. Fix-and-Flip (The Short Game: Capital Gains Focus)

This model involves acquiring undervalued, often distressed, properties, performing strategic renovations to rapidly increase value, and then selling them quickly for a profit. The goal is a fast turnaround and significant capital gain.

Strategic Considerations for Fix-and-Flip: This strategy requires a strong, active **buyer's market** where renovated homes sell quickly. You'll need **rehab expertise and management**, meaning reliable contractors for quality work, on budget and on time. Accurate budgeting is crucial; always add a 15-20% contingency.

Meticulously research comparable sales of recently renovated properties in the exact micro-market to determine a realistic **After Repair Value (ARV)**. Do not rely on projections. Remember that **holding costs are profit killers**; every month holding the property—taxes, insurance, utilities, loan interest—eats into profits, making quick sales essential. This model often involves hard money or private loans with higher interest rates and shorter terms, necessitating rapid execution through specific **loan structures**.

The **pros** of fix-and-flip include the potential for quick, significant profits, less long-term commitment, and the ability to generate capital rapidly for reinvestment. The **cons** are a higher risk profile, extreme susceptibility to market shifts, demanding contractor management and constant oversight, significant liquidity risk if the property doesn't sell quickly, and a high potential for unforeseen repair costs and budget overruns.

Defining Your Investment Niche: Property Types & Operational Models

Beyond the general investment models, you'll need to define your niche by choosing specific property types and operational models.

I. Traditional Residential Rental Investing (Core Property Types)

- **Single-Family Home Investing:** This involves acquiring individual houses for rental. It's often a good entry point due to simpler financing and management, with strong appreciation potential in some markets.
- **1-4 Unit Multi-Family Investing:** This covers duplexes, triplexes, and fourplexes. These are simpler to finance with residential loans, accessible for new investors, and offer diversified income streams and some economies of scale.
- **5+ Unit (Commercial) Multi-Family Investing:** This refers to larger apartment buildings, financed with commercial loans based on property income. They offer significant economies of scale, highly diversified income, and greater potential for forced appreciation, but require higher initial capital and more complex financing.

II. Specialized Residential Rental Niches (Exploring Specific Operational Models)

- **Section 8 Housing:** This involves renting to tenants with government-subsidized rent, offering stable, guaranteed payments but requiring rigorous inspections and specific management considerations.
- **Short-Term Rentals (e.g., Airbnb/VRBO):** These are nightly or weekly rentals with potentially higher income but significantly higher operational demands like cleaning, communication, and marketing, along with strict local regulations.

- **Renting Rooms / Room-by-Room Rentals:** Leasing individual rooms within a home often maximizes cash flow, caters to specific demographics like students or young professionals, and demands more intensive management.
- **Group Homes:** These are properties adapted and licensed for specific populations, such as individuals with disabilities or seniors. They can offer stable, high-income streams often backed by government programs but require specialized regulations, licensing, and expertise.

III. Commercial Real Estate Investing

- **Commercial Real Estate (Non-Residential):** This category includes retail spaces, office buildings, industrial warehouses, and mixed-use properties. These have different lease structures—often triple-net—tenant types, and risk profiles. They require specialized knowledge, a sophisticated support system, and significantly higher capital.

IV. Alternative Acquisition/Exit Strategies

- **Rent-to-Own:** Here, a tenant leases with an option to purchase. This provides upfront option money and consistent income, reducing vacancy, and appeals to tenants working towards homeownership.
- **Seller Financing:** In this scenario, the seller acts as the bank, which can be beneficial for sellers looking to offload quickly and buyers seeking alternative financing. It requires careful legal structuring.

Setting Your Non-Negotiables: The Strategic Filters

Your **non-negotiables** are your absolute deal-breakers – criteria that must be met for a property to even be considered. They prevent emotional decisions and wasted time.

Clearly define your **property condition** comfort level with work, setting your maximum acceptable rehab cost and type of work, such as "Turnkey," "Light Rehab," or "Heavy Rehab." Your chosen strategy dictates this.

For **neighborhood quality**, go beyond statistics to the lived reality. Set specific criteria for the block and surrounding area, perhaps a limit on boarded-up houses, proximity to amenities, or a minimum owner-occupancy rate.

Establish minimums for your **financial metrics**, defining your bottom line. This includes Cash-on-Cash Return (CoC), Capitalization Rate (Cap Rate), Maximum Price-to-Rent Ratio, or Maximum Debt-to-Income Ratio.

Specify your **property type** specialization, indicating the types of properties you will or won't invest in, such as "only single-family homes," "no commercial properties," or "minimum 3 bedrooms."

Finally, set strict rules for **due diligence findings**, with no compromises on verification. This includes essential checks like no open code violations, a clear title, verified tenant payment history, insurability, and no known lead paint unless abated.

Share these non-negotiables with your team and adhere to them with unwavering discipline. When a property fails even one, you walk away.

The Strategic Deal Vetting Process (Pre-Due Diligence Screening)

Before diving into forensic due diligence, your strategy provides an initial screening to efficiently filter out obvious non-starters.

Always prioritize **independent estimates over the seller's pro forma**. Never trust a seller's projected rent; instead, get verifiable comparables from local agents or property managers and cross-reference with online listings, focusing on actual rented properties. Get a rough rehab estimate from a reputable contractor, being skeptical of unrealistically low numbers. Model operating expenses conservatively, factoring in all costs like property management fees, utilities, landscaping, pest control, and significant maintenance reserves.

For **understanding market comps for the purchase price**, your independent real estate agent should provide comparable sales—properties recently sold within 3-6 months in the immediate area, of similar size, condition, and type. Crucially, focus exclusively on closed sales, as active listings or properties under contract only represent aspirations, not true market value. Compare apples to apples: distressed properties to other distressed sales; renovated properties to other renovated sales.

Be vigilant for **strategic red flags** during initial screening. These include "too high" projected rent or "too low" rehab estimates compared to the market, inconsistent numbers across a seller's portfolio, a lack of specificity, transparency, or refusal to provide details, high-pressure tactics and artificial scarcity, or no clear photos of key systems like the furnace, HVAC, electrical panel, roof, or basement.

This initial vetting is your first line of defense, ensuring only genuinely aligned opportunities move forward.

Developing Your Exit Strategy (Before You Enter) – The Escape Route

One of the most overlooked, yet strategically vital, aspects of a sound investment plan is the **exit plan**. Neglecting how you'll eventually divest can lead to being trapped or forced to sell at a loss.

Why Plan Your Exit from Day One? The Strategic Imperative

Planning your exit from day one ensures **comprehensive risk mitigation**, allowing you to proactively manage potential downsides like market shifts, declining values, or unexpected expenses. It enables **informed financial planning**, helping you understand long-term return potential and projected capital gains. A well-defined exit strategy also enhances **liquidity and flexibility**, improving your ability to adapt to changing circumstances. Finally, it ensures **market alignment and feasibility**, making sure your exit aligns with your chosen investment model and market realities.

Key Exit Options and Contingencies to Consider

Your **primary exit** might be a sale to another investor or homeowner. For a buy-and-hold strategy, consider at what appreciation level or after how many years you would sell. For a fix-and-flip, determine how quickly you need to sell to hit targets and what your backup plan is if it doesn't sell, such as renting it out.

Refinancing for cash-out can be part of your long-term strategy to acquire more properties or generate liquid capital. Understand eligibility for foreign investors. A **1031 Exchange (Tax-Deferred Exchange)** is a powerful tool to defer capital gains taxes when selling one investment property to acquire another "like-kind" property, but it requires strict adherence to IRS rules.

Always have **worst-case scenarios and contingency planning** in place. Have a clear understanding of your breaking point. How would you offload the property—even at a loss—to cut ties and preserve capital, perhaps through a quick sale to a cash buyer or a deed in lieu of foreclosure? This is your "Plan Z."

Your exit strategy isn't about hoping for the best; it's about being meticulously prepared for anything. It forces you to think about the entire lifecycle of the investment, building resilience and flexibility into your plan from the very beginning.

Strategy is an Ongoing Process, not a One-Time Setup – The Dynamic Blueprint

Your strategy is a living, breathing blueprint that must evolve with your experience, changing market conditions, and shifting personal goals. The market is dynamic; your strategy must be too.

Implement **regular review and adjustment cycles**. Schedule quarterly or annual reviews to assess if your goals are still relevant, if the market has shifted, or if your non-negotiables need refinement. This proactive review prevents obsolescence. Embrace **continuous learning and adaptation**, refining your strategy based on real-world feedback from successes and, more importantly, challenges. Every problem is a lesson. Finally, make sure to **leverage feedback from your support system**. Your property manager, agent, local advisor, attorney, and CPA are invaluable sources of real-time market intelligence. Use their insights to inform your strategic adjustments.

A clear, personalized, and dynamically managed strategy reduces complexity, minimizes costly missteps, and allows you to make data-driven decisions. It transforms you from a hopeful buyer into a confident, deliberate investor, ready to own your game and build a truly lasting legacy.

Reflection Pause:

Beyond just financial numbers, what are the core personal values or life goals that you want your real estate investments to support? How will your strategy explicitly reflect these, ensuring your investments align with your deepest purpose?

Which specific micro-market(s) are you now considering for your investments, and what three verifiable, hyper-local pieces of data (beyond general city statistics) define your interest in them? How will you confirm this data?

Based on your true risk tolerance and realistic time commitment, which investment model (e.g., cash flow buy-and-hold, fix-and-flip, or a niche strategy) aligns most realistically with your capabilities and goals, and why? What specific steps will you take to ensure this alignment?

Have you clearly defined your non-negotiables for property condition, neighborhood quality, and financial metrics? Write down at least five and commit to them.

What is your primary exit strategy for your next investment, and what are two contingency plans if that primary strategy doesn't unfold as expected?

Chapter 4: Structure

Building Your Protective Fortress

Your real estate isn't protected by its walls, but by the business built around it. That's your true fortress.

In "The Awakening," we fundamentally shifted your mindset, recognizing that real estate investing is a dynamic business, not a passive hobby. We then meticulously crafted your personalized Strategy in Chapter 3, defining your unique roadmap for purposeful investment, from micro-market selection to exit planning. You now understand the "what" and the "why" of your investment journey.

Now, we move to the second non-negotiable pillar: **Structure**.

As I often say, and it bears repeating: "The property is not the business. The property is a product. Your business is what protects it."

Let's shift gears from strategic planning to foundational building. By now, you've seen the ugly side of the game—the misinformation, the setup, the stress, and the devastating consequences of operating without foresight. You've seen what happens when intelligent, well-meaning individuals try to navigate the complex waters of U.S. real estate without a real, robust structure.

Now let's talk about what happens when you do it right. Because structure is not just about compliance; it's about protection, credibility, and the very longevity of your investment vision. You don't just need another property to add to a loose collection. You need a real, legitimate business entity behind every single deal, one that acts as a fortress around your assets and a shield for your personal wealth.

This Isn't a Side Hustle. This Is an *Operation*.

If you're buying U.S. real estate—especially from another country—you're not just a buyer. You are, by definition, a **business owner**. The moment you acquire that property, you assume the responsibilities, liabilities, and opportunities of running an enterprise. And if you don't treat it like one, with the formality and diligence it demands, you will consistently:

- Lose money through unexpected lawsuits, avoidable tax penalties, and inefficient operations.
- Remain reliant on others, at the mercy of your property manager or other service providers without your own systems.
- Operate in confusion, lacking clear financial records, legal boundaries, and operational procedures.
- Miss out on significant tax advantages due to improper structuring and inadequate record-keeping.
- Set yourself up to get burned by leaving your personal assets exposed and inviting exploitation.

Here's what most miseducated investors never hear: You can own 10 properties and still not have a business. You can have a sprawling portfolio that is nothing more than a collection of unmanaged liabilities. Or you can own just one—and run it like a million-dollar company, with precision, protection, and unparalleled efficiency. The difference lies entirely in your structural approach.

The 5 Pillars of Investor Structure: Your Unyielding Foundation

If you want to play the real game, if you want to build lasting wealth and a true legacy, these five pillars of investor structure are the non-negotiables. They are the essential components that transform a mere property into a protected, profitable, and scalable business operation.

1. Legal Entity Setup: Your Primary Shield

The era of buying property in your personal name, especially as an international investor, must end now. This is a fundamental error, a gaping hole in your defense. You need a U.S. legal entity—typically an LLC (Limited Liability Company), but sometimes a trust or a corporate structure—that is meticulously set up to fit your specific investment plan and your personal circumstances.

Why Your Name Should Never Be on the Deed: The Imperative of Legal Separation

The core reason for a legal entity is **asset protection**. When you own property in your personal name, there is no legal separation between your investment and your personal wealth. This means that if a lawsuit arises from the property—a tenant slips and falls, a contractor is injured, a city fine escalates, or a dispute arises with a neighbor—your personal assets (your home, your savings, your retirement funds, your other businesses, even your future earnings) are directly exposed. A judgment against the property can become a judgment against you, personally, across international borders.

A properly formed legal entity, like an LLC, creates a distinct legal person. The LLC owns the property, not you directly. Therefore, if a lawsuit occurs, the claim is generally against the LLC, and your personal liability is limited to the assets within that LLC. It's your primary shield, your first line of defense against unforeseen liabilities.

Beyond Protection: The Other Benefits of Entity Structure

Operating through a formal entity signals **credibility** to lenders, brokers, property managers, and even tenants. It shows you are a serious investor, not a hobbyist, which can open doors to better deals and more reliable partners.

While complex for foreign investors, a U.S. legal entity can offer significant **tax benefits**, including depreciation deductions, expense write-offs, and strategic tax planning opportunities not available to individuals. This, of course, requires careful consultation with a U.S. CPA specializing in foreign investment.

The **separation of personal and business assets** is crucial not just for liability, but for clarity. Keeping your personal finances separate from your investment business finances is essential for accurate accounting, easier auditing, and clear financial decision-making.

Lastly, an entity structure simplifies **succession planning**, making the transfer of ownership or management easier in the event of your incapacitation or death, ensuring your legacy is preserved according to your wishes.

Don't let anyone tell you entity setup is optional or an unnecessary expense. If you're investing across borders, it's not just essential; it's the cornerstone of responsible wealth building.

Case Study: The South African Family Who Owned a Disaster (Personally)

I had a client from South Africa—a husband, wife, and their adult daughter—who bought a duplex in a U.S. inner city. They were intelligent, diligent people, but they were miseducated on the fundamentals of U.S. real estate structure.

They did everything they thought was right based on the advice they received: they found a seemingly good deal online, promising high cash flow; they hired someone (recommended by the seller) to help them manage it; and, fatally, they put their personal names directly on the deed.

What they didn't do? Form a U.S. legal entity. No LLC. No asset protection. No corporate structure. They believed the property itself was the investment, not realizing the business behind the property was what truly mattered. And it cost them—badly.

When I got involved, here's what I walked into, a situation that perfectly illustrates the peril of lacking proper structure:

First, a squatter was living inside the property. Upon closing, this property was far from the occupied duplex I'd anticipated. Instead, I found one unit vacant and vandalized, and the other occupied by a squatter left behind by the previous owner. The squatter had taken over the downstairs unit, meaning no rent, active property damage, and a legal nightmare to remove them.

Second, a busted pipe was running unchecked. Due to the squatter and the absentee management, a pipe in the upstairs vandalized unit had burst, and water had been running for weeks, perhaps months, undetected. This caused extensive structural damage, mold growth, and a horrific utility bill.

Then came a $50,000 water bill waiting in the mailbox. The unchecked pipe resulted in an astronomical water bill, a debt attached directly to the property and, by extension, to the personal names on the deed.

Finally, the property faced condemnation. After we finally managed to get the squatter evicted (a lengthy and costly legal process), the city came out, inspected the water-damaged, mold-ridden home, and condemned it on the spot. This meant it was legally unsafe for occupancy, could not be rented, and required massive, expensive repairs to be habitable again.

So now you've got a foreign family with no property access, a condemned asset, and a five-figure utility bill—all legally attached to their personal names. That meant their personal credit, their financial identity, and their entire legal exposure were on the line. Their personal bank accounts, their home back in South Africa possibly, their businesses—all potentially within reach of a U.S. lawsuit or debt collection.

All because no one told them: "This isn't just a property—it's a liability without structure." They didn't have protection. They didn't have legal separation. And they didn't have a single layer of insulation between their investment and their family's entire financial well-being.

Moral of the story? If you're buying in the U.S., you need a U.S. entity. Not tomorrow. Not next year. Now. Because it's not a matter of if something will go wrong. It's a matter of when. And when it does, your LLC becomes your first line of defense—not your passport, not your apology, and certainly not your personal bank account.

Practical Steps for Legal Entity Setup as an International Investor:

The most crucial step is to **consult a U.S. Attorney** specializing in corporate law and foreign investment. They will advise on the best entity type for your specific needs (LLC, C-Corp, etc.), considering your tax situation and home country.

Next, you'll **choose your state of formation**. While some investors choose states like Delaware or Wyoming for perceived privacy or asset protection, it's often simpler to form the LLC in the state where your property is located. If you form it elsewhere, you'll likely need to register it as a "foreign LLC" in the property's state, incurring additional fees and compliance.

Your attorney or CPA can help you **obtain an EIN** (Employer Identification Number) from the IRS. This is essential for your U.S. business bank account and tax filings.

A critical document, to be prepared by your attorney, is the **Operating Agreement**. This outlines the rules of your LLC, including ownership, management, profit distribution, and what happens in various scenarios.

Finally, every LLC must **appoint a Registered Agent** in the state of formation—a physical address to receive legal and tax documents. This can be a service or your attorney.

2. Business Banking: Your Property's Own Financial Identity

Once you've established your legal entity, the next critical move is setting up your U.S. business bank account—in that company's name. This is not merely a convenience; it is a non-negotiable pillar of sound financial structure.

Why Your Property Needs Its Own Financial Identity

This is how real investors operate with transparency, accountability, and efficiency. A dedicated business bank account allows you to:

- **Collect rent legally and transparently:** All rental income flows directly into the business account, creating a clear audit trail.
- **Pay vendors and contractors efficiently:** All property-related expenses are paid from this account, simplifying expense tracking.
- **Track every dollar in and out:** This is paramount for accurate bookkeeping, tax preparation, and understanding your true profitability.
- **Maintain clean books for taxes, audits, and lenders:** Separate accounts mean no commingling, which is vital for legal protection and financial clarity.
- **Start building business credit:** Over time, consistent, responsible financial activity through your business account can help establish business credit, potentially enabling future financing opportunities.

More importantly, this is how you make your investment real and professional. Because until your money has a home inside a real business account, you're not running a company. You're running a side hustle on hope, vulnerable to confusion and exploitation.

Separate the Money. Always.

One of the biggest, most common, and most dangerous mistakes I see foreign investors make is this: They collect rent in their personal foreign account. Or worse—some property manager sends it to them through a random transfer app, like PayPal or Western Union, with no clear paper trail, no consistent reporting, and no accountability. That's not business. That's confusion, a legal and financial disaster waiting to happen.

Your U.S. business account should be:

- **In your U.S. LLC or entity name**, clearly linking all financial activity to your protected legal entity.
- **Used only for that property or portfolio**, avoiding mixing funds from different properties unless they are under the same multi-property LLC.
- **Cleanly separated from personal or foreign income**, reinforcing the legal separation of your LLC and simplifying tax reporting.
- **Accessible online**, with robust reporting features, allowing you to monitor transactions, download statements, and track cash flow from anywhere in the world.
- **Able to issue and receive various payment types**, including wire transfers, ACH (Automated Clearing House) payments, and checks in your company name, facilitating seamless operations with U.S. vendors and tenants.

But I'm Not a U.S. Citizen—Can I Still Open One? Yes.

This is a common concern, and while it can be challenging, it is absolutely possible. There are foreign investor-friendly banks that work specifically with non-citizens and non-residents. Some traditional banks may require a physical visit to the U.S. to open the account, which can be coordinated with an investment trip. Others have specialized international divisions or digital onboarding processes that may allow you to open an account remotely, often with the help of your U.S. attorney or registered agent. The key is to find the right institution that understands and caters to foreign investors.

Because without a proper U.S. business bank account:

- You can't hire real, professional vendors who require formal payment methods.
- You can't automate systems like rent collection or bill payments, increasing operational burden.

- You can't build business credit, limiting future financing options.
- You can't clearly show cash flow or financial performance to potential lenders or partners.
- And you look unprofessional—even to your own team, who may view you as less serious or more prone to disorganization.

Think Like a Business, Bank Like a Business. Your rent income? That's revenue. Your repair expenses? That's cost of goods sold. Your property taxes and insurance? That's overhead. So why would you run all that through your personal debit card or a messy P2P payment app? If you want real estate to pay you like a business, you must run it like one. That starts with how you handle the money.

3. Accounting + Bookkeeping Systems: If You Can't Track It, You Can't Grow It

Let's be brutally real—if you can't produce a clear, accurate Profit and Loss statement (P&L) for each property you own, or for your overall portfolio, you're not investing. You're guessing. You're hoping you're profitable. You're hoping you're cash flowing. You're hoping the numbers work out in your favor. But hope isn't a system. And in real estate, what you don't track will inevitably cost you, often in devastating ways.

Why Bookkeeping Isn't Optional: It's Business Infrastructure

This isn't busywork. This is essential business infrastructure. You need a robust, consistent system for tracking every financial transaction—not a haphazard spreadsheet someone made in Google Drive at 2 a.m. Not a jumble of receipts stuffed in an inbox or scattered across WhatsApp messages from your property manager. Not vague statements like "I think we made around $800 this month." That's not how serious, protected investors operate.

Here's what you actually need to implement:

You need **detailed monthly reports**: consistent, comprehensive breakdowns that show all income, all expenses, and the net cash flow per property—every single month, with no excuses or delays. These reports should be generated from a dedicated accounting system, not manually compiled.

Granular expense tracking is paramount. Every dollar spent must be tracked down to the penny, including all repairs (large and small), property management fees, property taxes, insurance premiums, utilities (if landlord-paid), contractor payouts, legal fees, and any other operational costs. You should be able to see every dollar that leaves your business and precisely why it left.

Don't overlook **depreciation schedules and asset management**. You're leaving significant money on the table if you're not leveraging depreciation. Depreciation is a non-cash expense that reduces your taxable income, effectively increasing your after-tax cash flow. A solid depreciation strategy, managed by a qualified CPA, can significantly reduce your U.S. tax burden and increase your effective ROI—legally and strategically. This requires proper asset classification and tracking.

A **real estate–savvy U.S. CPA or Tax Advisor** is a critical component of your Support System and your structural integrity. You need a U.S. tax professional who:

- Deeply understands U.S. real estate tax laws and their specific application to rental properties.
- Specializes in working with foreign and non-resident investors, navigating complex international tax treaties and reporting requirements.
- Knows how to file the right forms (like IRS Form 1040NR for non-resident individuals, Form 1120-F for foreign corporations,

FBAR for foreign bank accounts, and understands FIRPTA rules for property sales).

- Can help you legally reduce your U.S. tax burden through strategic deductions, depreciation, and entity structuring.
- Prepares you for the long-term implications of your investing activity, not just the annual tax season. They should be a proactive advisor, not just a reactive preparer.

This isn't about finding the cheapest tax preparer. It's about building a sophisticated financial team that helps you preserve, protect, and legally multiply your money, ensuring compliance and maximizing your net returns.

Stop Operating in the Dark: Gain Visibility and Control

When your books are clean, meticulously organized, and consistently updated, you gain unparalleled visibility into your investment business. This visibility translates directly into control and strategic advantage:

- You can quickly **spot financial leaks**, identifying where money is being overspent, where expenses are unexpectedly high, or where income is underperforming.
- You'll **identify true profitability**, knowing precisely which properties are truly profitable and which might be draining resources, allowing for data-driven decisions on holding, selling, or optimizing.
- Clean, verifiable financial statements are essential to **prove income to lenders and investors**, for securing future financing or attracting legitimate investment partners.
- Consistent reporting allows you to **spot trends before they become problems**—such as rising maintenance costs or increasing vacancies—enabling proactive intervention before they escalate into major crises.

- Your decisions become **data-driven**, based on verifiable facts and figures, not gut feelings, hopes, or misleading sales pitches.
- You can **defend your business with confidence**. If the IRS audits you, if a city files a lien, if a partner wants to see returns, or if you face a legal challenge, you'll have every transaction, every expense, and every dollar accounted for in black and white. You're prepared, not scrambling.

You're Not Just a Buyer. You're a Business Owner. Real estate isn't just about the asset itself. It's fundamentally about the operation that surrounds and protects that asset. And accounting is the precise language your business speaks. If you're not tracking it, you're not protecting it. And if you're not protecting it, you're certainly not ready to scale it.

4. Insurance + Risk Management: Because One Lawsuit Can Wipe Out Everything You Built

Let's kill the dangerous assumption right now: you don't just need *any* insurance—you need the *right* insurance. The kind that meticulously protects your physical property, your rental income (in case of vacancy due to covered perils), your legal liability (if someone is injured on your property), and, crucially, your personal name and financial well-being.

This isn't something you put off, cheap out on, or assume your property manager has fully handled. Because the day something goes wrong—and again, in real estate, it's not an if, but a when—your carefully chosen policy is either your impenetrable shield or your deafening silence in the face of financial ruin.

Case Study: The Lawsuit That Caught Her Off Guard (and Uninsured)

One of my clients, an international investor, owned a duplex she was ready to offload. The property was in a challenging inner-city market, and the downstairs unit had already been hit with a lead abatement order from the city, meaning it couldn't legally be rented until expensive environmental work was done. Her best financial move was to sell the property quickly and cut her losses.

A buyer came forward, and they scheduled the home inspection. During that inspection, the inspector casually mentioned that the basement stairs needed reinforcement—a minor structural note. The upstairs tenant, who was present during part of the inspection, unfortunately overheard this comment.

Two days later, that same tenant "fell" down the basement stairs. He immediately filed a six-figure lawsuit, claiming severe injuries due to the landlord's negligence in maintaining safe premises.

My client had no landlord insurance. She was caught completely off guard, because she was selling the house and let her policy lapse. Not only did she lose the pending sale, but she was now facing a devastating legal nightmare—personally liable for a six-figure claim because she didn't have the right protections in place. The lawsuit dragged on, costing her immense legal fees, emotional stress, and ultimately, a significant settlement that directly impacted her personal finances.

And all of this could've been prevented with a basic landlord policy and general liability coverage. It was an avoidable disaster, a direct consequence of a gaping hole in her Structure.

What the Right Insurance Actually Looks Like for an Investor

Here's what you need to have—no matter what, and always reviewed by your U.S. insurance broker specializing in rental properties:

You need **Landlord Policies** (Dwelling Fire/Rental Dwelling Policies). This is not a regular homeowner's policy; it's specifically designed for income properties, including:

- **Property Coverage:** Protects the physical structure from perils like fire, wind, hail, and sometimes vandalism.
- **Tenant Liability Coverage:** Protects you if a tenant or their guest is injured on your property and you are found negligent. This is the most critical component for a landlord.
- **Loss of Rents/Fair Rental Value Coverage:** Replaces lost rental income if the property becomes uninhabitable due to a covered peril (e.g., fire).
- **Legal Defense:** Covers your legal fees if you are sued by a tenant or third party.

Be aware of **vacancy protection**. Many standard landlord policies become void if your unit is sitting empty for more than 30 or 60 days. You need specific coverage or an endorsement that accounts for extended vacancy—especially crucial during extensive renovations, prolonged tenant transitions, or challenging market conditions.

Aim for **high liability limits**. Inner-city homes, due to their age and sometimes challenging environments, can be at higher risk for various incidents. You need strong liability limits—$300,000 minimum, but preferably $500,000 to $1,000,000 per occurrence.

Umbrella Coverage is an additional, crucial layer of liability protection that extends across all your properties and across multiple claims, typically providing $1 million or more in additional coverage above your primary landlord policies. It's how smart investors keep catastrophic lawsuits from touching their personal wealth. It acts as an overarching shield.

If you're undertaking significant renovations or flips, a standard landlord policy may not cover the property during construction. **Builder's Risk or Renovation Policies** are required to protect the property and materials during the construction phase.

Finally, if you are actively involved in advising other investors, managing properties for others, or engaging in complex real estate transactions beyond just owning your own rentals, you may need **Professional Liability (E&O)** insurance to protect against claims of professional negligence.

What's at Risk Without It? Everything.

One fall by a tenant or visitor. One devastating fire. One angry tenant filing a frivolous but costly lawsuit. One contractor accident on your property. One squatter incident leading to significant damage and legal fees.

And suddenly your entire portfolio, your business bank account, and your personal wealth are exposed. Insurance is not about fear. It's about strategy—a proactive, calculated decision to mitigate predictable risks. Because if your asset isn't protected, your income isn't either. And real investors never let their hard-earned wealth ride unprotected.

5. Documentation + Systems: Your Investment Is Only as Strong as Your Receipts

Let's make something crystal clear: you don't need WhatsApp threads as your primary record-keeping. You don't need random screenshots or scattered emails as your audit trail. You need robust, centralized, and accessible systems.

Because when the city calls with a violation, when a tenant sues, when your property manager ghosts, when a deal goes sideways, or when the IRS audits you—you won't magically rise to the occasion. You'll fall to your level of documentation. And if that level is disorganized and incomplete, you will lose.

This Is the Backbone of Your Operation: Protection and Proof

Systems don't just organize your business; they protect it. They prove it. They give it structure, memory, and resilience—especially when you're operating from across the globe and relying on others.

Here's what that looks like in practice:

Property Management Agreements (PMAs) must be signed, detailed, and dated. They are your contract with your property manager, spelling out their exact roles, responsibilities, fees, expectations for communication and reporting, and clear terms for termination. If your manager disappears or underperforms and you have nothing in writing, you have no legal leverage—just a frustrating story.

Every single tenant issue or repair request should be meticulously documented in **maintenance request logs**: date received, time addressed, detailed description of the issue, cost of repair, vendor used, before-and-after photos, and tenant sign-off (if possible). If a tenant ever files a claim or says, "I told you the leak wasn't fixed," your detailed log is your indisputable defense.

You need fully executed **lease files**, with no verbal agreements. No "I think they pay $950." This includes move-in checklists, security deposit forms, clear rent schedules, and all necessary legal addendums—especially crucial for Section 8 tenants or properties involved in city programs with specific compliance requirements.

Before you buy, you need a standardized, comprehensive **due diligence checklist & reports** that documents every step of your due diligence: title review, utility status, lead registry search, code enforcement report, lease verification, neighborhood analysis, inspection reports, and financial projections. Having a consistent checklist saves you from emotion-driven purchases and blind spots, ensuring no critical step is missed.

Every rehab or major repair project needs a clear, detailed paper trail in **Scope of Work (SOW) folders & rehab documentation**. This means the line-item bid from the contractor, before-and-after photos of the work, copies of all necessary permits, detailed invoices for materials and labor, and receipts. Document who did what and when. So, if a new manager steps in, or a city inspector asks questions, you have the full, verifiable story, not just someone else's vague version of it.

Inspection reports—whether city-mandated, lender-required appraisals, or self-ordered property condition assessments—are your early-warning radar. Get them done, read them thoroughly, and save them. They help you plan repairs, budget capital expenditures, and protect tenants legally by identifying hazards.

Finally, your critical files should live in a secure, **cloud-based storage and centralized system**, not scattered across someone's laptop, a local hard drive, or disparate email accounts. Whatever you use—make it accessible, consistent, and secure. Grant your trusted Support System members access to what they need, without handing over your entire digital empire.

No Systems? No Proof. No Power.

When something inevitably goes wrong—and it will—you don't want to be the investor scrambling to pull receipts from fragmented text threads, asking your contractor to "resend that invoice from six months ago," or begging your property manager for a report they never sent.

You want to be the one who says, with calm confidence, "Here's the executed lease." "Here's the maintenance log for that issue." "Here's the permit for that renovation." "Here's the full financial file, audited and ready."

Documentation beats conversation. Systems turn chaos into clarity. And that's how real investors move. That's how they protect their assets, defend their decisions, and ultimately, build lasting wealth.

The Goal Is Not More Deals. It's Better Decisions.

Anybody can buy another property. The market is full of cheap houses, eager sellers, and aggressive wholesalers. But can you:

- Track performance across your entire portfolio with precision?
- Spot leaks in your operational process before they become devastating losses?
- Hand off your entire operation to a new team member and know it will run seamlessly without your constant intervention?
- Confidently defend your asset if a tenant sues, a contractor flakes, a fire hits, or the IRS comes knocking?

That's what structure gives you. It's not just paperwork. It's power. It's the ability to operate with confidence, clarity, and control, transforming your investment from a series of isolated transactions into a cohesive, protected, and scalable business.

Real Investors Build Companies—Not Just Portfolios

Because when your investment business is structured right:

- You can **scale with confidence**: Adding new properties becomes a systematic process, not a chaotic gamble, because your foundational systems are already in place.

- You can **attract legitimate partners and lenders**: A well-structured business with clean books and clear legal entities is far more appealing to serious investors, private lenders, and traditional banks.
- You can **qualify for better financing**: Banks prefer to lend to established, well-organized entities with verifiable financial histories.
- You can **pursue larger opportunities**, perhaps even city contracts for housing rehabilitation or private lender deals, which are often reserved for established businesses.
- You can **move like a CEO, not just a buyer**: You are directing an operation, making strategic decisions based on data and protection, rather than reacting emotionally to individual problems.

And that's the ultimate point. Your real estate should be a business. Because a business, properly structured, has protection, leverage, and longevity. It is the vehicle through which your investment Strategy is executed, and your long-term legacy is built.

Reflection Check-In:

Are You Building a Fortress or a House of Cards?

As you conclude this chapter on Structure, take a moment to honestly assess your current approach or your plans for your next investment.

1. **Legal Entity:** Do you currently own, or plan to own, U.S. property in your personal name? If so, what immediate steps will you take to consult with a U.S. attorney about forming a protective legal entity (e.g., LLC)? What specific questions will you ask them?
2. **Business Banking:** Do you have a dedicated U.S. business bank account in the name of your legal entity, used *only* for your investment activities? If not, what actions will you take

this week to explore opening one, and what potential challenges do you foresee as a foreign investor?

3. **Accounting & Bookkeeping:** Can you instantly generate a clean, accurate Profit and Loss statement for each of your properties or your overall portfolio for the last 12 months? If not, what specific accounting system or professional will you implement to gain this critical financial visibility?
4. **Insurance & Risk Management:** Have you reviewed your current insurance policies with a U.S. broker specializing in rental properties to ensure you have comprehensive landlord liability, adequate coverage for physical property, and umbrella coverage? What are the top three potential risks you're currently exposed to if your insurance is insufficient?
5. **Documentation & Systems:** Where do your critical investment documents currently reside (e.g., leases, PMAs, inspection reports, repair logs)? What is one immediate action you can take to centralize and secure this documentation in a cloud-based system, making it accessible and auditable?

Remember, the goal is not merely to acquire properties, but to build a robust, protected, and scalable business. Your structure is the foundation of that business.

Chapter 5: Support

Assembling Your Indispensable Ground Crew

If you want to go fast, go alone. If you want to go far, go together.

In "The Awakening," you shifted your mindset from a passive observer to a strategic participant, understanding that real estate is a dynamic business. In "Strategy," we meticulously crafted your personalized blueprint, defining your unique roadmap for purposeful investment. And in "Structure," you learned how to fortify your assets with an unyielding legal and financial framework, recognizing that your business, not just the property, is what truly protects your vision.

Now, we arrive at the third, and for the international investor, arguably the most vital pillar: **Support**.

You can possess the most brilliant **Strategy** for identifying profitable deals. You can establish the most robust **Structure** to protect your assets and optimize your taxes. But if you lack a reliable, trustworthy **Support** system—a meticulously vetted, multi-layered network of professionals and trusted advisors on the ground—your investment is still a ship adrift without a compass, vulnerable to every storm. Distance, in this game, is not just geographical; it's a profound vulnerability that only genuine, on-the-ground support can bridge. This support acts as your proxy, your intelligence network, and your ultimate accountability check, ensuring that your strategic vision is executed and your structural protections are maintained, even when you are thousands of miles away.

The Isolation Trap: The Peril of Operating Alone (and Blind)

The allure of remote investing is undeniably strong: the promise of managing your portfolio from the comfort of your home country, collecting seemingly passive income, and avoiding the perceived day-to-day hassles of property ownership. This attractive promise, however, often leads investors into a dangerous "isolation trap"—a delusion that once the money is wired and a property manager is nominally in place, their work is done. This couldn't be further from the truth, and it's a mistake that has cost countless international investors their capital, their peace of mind, and their entire investment dreams.

Operating without a true, multi-layered support system means you are operating blind, exposed, and ultimately, powerless. This results in profound blind spots, as you cannot physically see the subtle signs of property neglect, the true condition of a property (beyond curated photos or staged virtual tours), or the constantly shifting dynamics of a neighborhood. You are forced to rely solely on reports and images that can be easily manipulated, selectively provided, or entirely incomplete. This leaves you vulnerable to deteriorating assets, missed opportunities, and escalating problems that you simply cannot detect from afar. You're essentially trying to navigate a complex, ever-changing landscape with your eyes closed, relying on someone else's potentially skewed vision.

This isolation also leads to exacerbated problems and delayed reactions. Geographical distance inherently means delayed reactions. A minor leaky pipe, if unreported or ignored, quickly becomes a catastrophic flooded basement. A single missed rent payment spirals into a months-long, emotionally and financially draining eviction process. Small, manageable issues, which could be resolved quickly and cheaply with immediate, competent intervention, become massive, costly crises because of a lack of timely awareness and proactive problem-solving from the ground. Time is money, and in real estate, delayed action is almost always synonymous with escalating costs and diminished returns.

Furthermore, you experience extreme vulnerability to fraud and incompetence. Unscrupulous individuals, opportunistic con artists, and even well-meaning but utterly incompetent partners thrive on the geographical and informational distance. They know you can't easily verify their claims, inspect their work, or hold them directly accountable in person. They can overcharge for phantom repairs, claim properties are occupied when they're vacant, or simply neglect your asset while continuing to bill you for non-existent services. Even without malicious intent, incompetent support can cause significant, irreversible damage if left unchecked, turning your promising investment into a constant source of frustration, unexpected expense, and ultimately, a complete financial drain.

The consequence is a crushing emotional and financial drain. The constant anxiety of not knowing what's truly happening with your investment, the frustration of unanswered calls and vague reports, and the despair of seeing your hard-earned capital vanish into a black hole of unexpected expenses can be emotionally crippling. This sustained emotional toll often leads to extreme stress, burnout, and ultimately, a complete abandonment of the investment, liquidating assets at a loss just to regain peace of mind and escape the nightmare. The "passive income" dream morphs into an active, debilitating nightmare of worry and regret.

Finally, operating without a robust support system leads to a total loss of control. Without a reliable team that operates with transparency, integrity, and accountability, you effectively cede control of your investment to others. You become a passive passenger in your own financial journey, merely observing events rather than actively driving outcomes. You might not realize the extent of your vulnerability until a major crisis hits, and by then, the damage is often already done, and reversing course is monumentally difficult and expensive. Your investment becomes a liability that controls you, rather than an asset you control.

Consider the harrowing story of a client from the Middle East, a retired oil executive named Omar. Omar had spent his career managing complex international operations, so he understood the importance of delegation and building effective teams. He was drawn to U.S. real estate as a way to secure his retirement, seeing it as a stable, long-term asset. He found a "full-service investment company" online that promised to handle everything from acquisition to renovation and ongoing property management in St. Louis. They assured him he'd never need to visit the U.S., painting a picture of effortless, truly passive income.

Omar's Strategy was clear: acquire three single-family rentals, renovate them to a high standard, and enjoy steady cash flow. He had even established an LLC for his investments, demonstrating a basic understanding of Structure to protect his personal assets. But his primary structural weakness, and ultimately his downfall, was his complete reliance on a single, unvetted company for all his Support needs. He trusted them implicitly, believing their "full-service" promise meant they were his infallible eyes and ears on the ground, eliminating any need for his own vigilance.

For the first few months, Omar received glossy, professional-looking reports and consistent rent payments directly into his U.S. bank account. He felt confident, even elated, that he had found the perfect solution for remote investing. Then, subtly at first, the reports became less frequent, and the rent payments grew sporadic, often accompanied by vague explanations of "tenant issues" or "unexpected repairs." When he tried to call his primary contact at the company, the phone often went straight to voicemail. Emails were met with vague excuses or no response at all for days, sometimes weeks.

Omar's unease grew into a deep suspicion. He asked for updated, timestamped photos of the properties. The company sent him pictures that looked suspiciously similar to the ones from months ago, or even from the initial listing. He requested detailed invoices for increasingly high "repair" charges he was being billed, but they were often vague, lacked specifics, or were outright missing. He was paying for routine maintenance, but his tenants (whom he eventually managed to contact directly through desperate online searches for his property addresses) complained about a litany of unresolved issues: a persistent leaky faucet, a broken furnace in winter, a collapsing section of the fence, and even mice infestations.

The real shock came when he decided to hire an independent inspector and a local real estate agent to visit his properties for an independent appraisal. What they found was horrifying. One house, supposedly "fully renovated" and tenanted, had a gaping hole in the roof that had been poorly covered with a tarp, leading to severe water damage throughout the attic and upper floor. It was clearly uninhabitable, yet he was still being charged management fees. Another property, listed as "tenant-occupied" and generating income, was completely vacant and boarded up, with signs of extensive vandalism and copper pipe theft. The third property did indeed have a tenant, but the interior was in severe disrepair, and the tenant claimed she hadn't seen the property manager in months and was rightfully escrowing rent due to unaddressed major maintenance requests that had made the unit unsafe.

Omar had been paying for repairs that never happened and for management of properties that were actively deteriorating, sometimes to dangerous levels. The "full-service" company was a sophisticated facade, simply collecting his money and neglecting his assets, bleeding them dry while projecting a flawless image. His initial Strategy was sound, and his Structure was in place, but his complete lack of independent, on-the-ground Support meant he was operating in a vacuum, completely vulnerable to deceit and negligence. He had delegated, but he hadn't created a system for oversight or verification, assuming trust where none was earned. He was paying for peace of mind but receiving a recurring nightmare that drained his savings and threatened his retirement.

Build the Team BEFORE You Need Them: Your Proactive Defense

You've probably heard the saying: "If you want to go fast, go alone. If you want to go far, go together." Well, real estate will humble you quickly if you try to go fast, alone. Especially in the U.S.—and critically, especially from overseas—your success will live or die by the strength, integrity, and proactive nature of your team.

Because once the property is yours, the game fundamentally shifts from acquisition to operations. And operations are handled by people.

This is not e-commerce. This is not crypto. This is not "buy it and sit on it." This is about contractors showing up and completing quality work, property managers communicating transparently and proactively, tenants following lease terms and paying rent consistently, inspectors passing your properties for occupancy and compliance, vendors getting paid accurately and on time, cities issuing permits and not levying fines, attorneys closing deals smoothly and handling legal issues effectively, CPAs filing taxes correctly and strategically, and lenders underwriting loans favorably. And every single one of those outcomes is tied to a person, a relationship, and a system of accountability. If your relationships are weak, if your team is unvetted, or if your oversight is lacking, your entire operation is weak—no matter how good the deal looked on paper.

One of the worst mistakes new investors make is waiting until there's a fire to go looking for a fire extinguisher. You don't find an attorney after you've been sued. You don't go contractor-hunting when your rehab is halfway done and stalled. You don't hire a new property manager after your tenant ghosts, and your property gets trashed. You don't Google "insurance coverage" after the house catches fire.

You build your bench before game day. Because when things go left—and they will, it's an inevitability in real estate—the only thing standing between your money and a meltdown is the strength, competence, and trustworthiness of your team.

Let me tell you how I learned this the hard way, and why it became the driving force behind this book. This isn't theory for me. This is personal. For years, this is exactly how I got most of my foreign clients: after the fire. I wasn't the one they called to help them grow their portfolio strategically. I was the one they called to clean up the devastating mess.

They'd find me after they got burned by a fraudulent wholesaler, after their "property manager" disappeared with months of rent, or after they realized the house they bought was in housing court, or had a squatter, or was racking up $50 a day in city fines for violations they didn't even know existed.

And every single time, I'd drop what I was doing, step in, and try to fix it. Get the squatter out. Get the violations cleared. Coordinate the complex, often expensive, rehab. Figure out what happened and why. And honestly? It wore me out. It was emotionally and financially draining, not just for the clients, but for me.

Because these weren't just bad deals. They were avoidable disasters. Disasters that wouldn't have happened if someone had simply taught them: Build the team before you need them. Not after the lawsuit. Not after the leak. Not after the $50,000 water bill. Not after the tenant fell down the stairs and filed a six-figure claim.

I wrote this book out of pure obedience. If I'm honest, it's not one I wanted to write because I don't want any enemies. But I couldn't stand seeing good people—often with substantial savings and the best intentions—get destroyed by a fundamental lack of preparation and proper guidance. What truly broke my heart was that they weren't foolish or greedy; they were simply miseducated. They put their trust in the wrong people because they didn't know who the right ones were or how to vet them effectively.

So, God told me I had to be the one to say what no one else was saying, and I'm sure it will ruffle some feathers. I anticipate some people will come for me, although I genuinely don't want any smoke from this fire. My intention is simply to put out the fire once and for all. This chapter? Consider it your warning and your ultimate weapon. If you take its message seriously now, if you proactively build your support system, you'll dodge the exact pain that brought 90% of my clients to my doorstep. Don't wait. Build your team now. That way, when the pressure hits and the inevitable challenges arise, you'll have dependable people—not panic.

Key Elements of a Strong Support System: Your Ground Crew

A robust support system is far more than just hiring a property manager. It's building a multi-layered network of trusted, meticulously vetted professionals who act as your informed eyes, vigilant ears, and capable hands on the ground. They are your intelligence network, your problem-solvers, and your essential accountability partners, ensuring your investment is nurtured, protected, and aligned with your Strategy and Structure.

Here's who should be on your U.S. Real Estate Team:

First, your **Property Manager: Your Day-to-Day Operator and First Line of Defense**. Their role is your primary operational contact. They handle tenant screening, lease enforcement, rent collection, maintenance coordination, financial reporting, and legal compliance (e.g., evictions). They are your direct link to the property and its occupants. It's crucial to remember they are not miracle workers. When looking for a property manager, verify they are properly licensed in the state where your property is located (if required by state law). They must have deep experience in your specific asset type (single-family, multi-family, Section 8) and, crucially, in your micro-market. Transparency is paramount; they must provide clear, detailed, and consistent monthly financial reports with supporting invoices, rent rolls, and maintenance logs, with no hidden fees or vague charges. They must also operate within all local, state, and federal landlord-tenant laws and fair housing regulations. Look for responsiveness and proactiveness, meaning they should communicate promptly, address issues before they escalate, and provide proactive updates, not just react to your inquiries. Finally, inquire about their rigorous tenant screening process (credit checks, background checks, employment verification, previous landlord references), as this is paramount to avoiding problem tenants.

Second, your **Real Estate Attorney: Your Legal Strategist and Shield**. Their role is not just someone who "does closings," but your legal strategist. They draft and review all contracts (purchase agreements, property management agreements, contractor agreements), handle evictions and legal notices, advise on entity structuring (as discussed in Chapter 4), and protect you from liability. When selecting an attorney, ensure they specialize in real estate law, and ideally, have significant experience working with foreign investors and the unique challenges they face (e.g., FIRPTA, international jurisdiction). They should be a proactive advisor, not just reactive, anticipating legal risks and advising on preventative measures. Clear, concise communication is also essential, explaining complex legal concepts in an understandable way.

Third, your **Contractor / Handyman: Your Asset Preservation Crew**. These are the individuals who perform repairs, maintenance, and renovations, critical for preserving your asset's value and ensuring tenant satisfaction. It is absolutely non-negotiable that they are properly licensed and insured (general liability and worker's compensation) in your state and municipality, demand proof. They must provide detailed, written scopes of work for all projects, outlining materials, timelines, and costs. They must also be willing to pull all required city permits for renovations, ensuring work is up to code and avoiding future fines. When vetting, do not rely solely on your property manager's recommendation; get multiple bids and vet them independently (check references, online reviews, past work). Always insist on milestone-based payments, never paying 100% upfront.

Fourth, your **CPA or Tax Advisor: Your Financial Navigator**. This professional manages your U.S. tax compliance, optimizes your tax position, and advises on the financial implications of your investment strategy. They must specialize in working with foreign and non-resident investors, understanding the intricacies of FIRPTA, effectively connected income, tax treaties, and specific IRS forms (e.g., 1040NR, 1120-F, FBAR). They should help you legally reduce your U.S. tax exposure through strategic deductions, depreciation, and entity structuring, not just prepare your annual returns, and advise on the long-term tax implications of your investing activity, including exit strategies.

Fifth, your **Bookkeeper or Financial Analyst: Your Data Steward**. This individual (or service) meticulously tracks all income and expenses, reconciles bank accounts, and generates accurate financial reports (P&L, balance sheets) for each property and your overall portfolio. Look for familiarity with common real estate expenses and accounting principles, proficiency with cloud-based accounting software (e.g., QuickBooks Online, Xero) and/or property management accounting modules. They should be able to provide clear, easy-to-understand reports on a monthly or quarterly basis, demonstrating meticulous attention to detail in tracking every penny.

Sixth, your **Insurance Broker: Your Risk Protector**. They help you secure the right insurance policies to protect your property, income, and liability. They must specialize in landlord policies, understanding the unique risks associated with income properties (e.g., tenant liability, loss of rents, specific perils in inner-city areas). Look for their ability to bundle policies (e.g., landlord and umbrella) for comprehensive coverage and potential savings. They should accurately assess risks related to lead paint, fire, vandalism, and specific neighborhood exposures, and clearly explain what your policy actually doesn't cover, so there are no surprises.

Finally, your **Local Inspector or Field Partner: Your Independent Eyes and Ears**. This is a crucial, often overlooked, layer of independent oversight. This could be a professional home inspector you hire for periodic checks, or a local, trusted partner (not involved in the deal itself) who acts as your "boots on the ground." Their independence is absolutely critical; they must have no financial ties to your seller, property manager, or contractor. Their job is to verify what you're being told by other members of your team. They walk properties, take real-time photo/video reports, and provide unbiased assessments of condition and work quality, providing proactive reporting that keeps you from relying on blind trust, offering an independent layer of accountability.

Proximity Doesn't Equal Loyalty: Vetting Your Team with Rigor

Just because someone's local doesn't mean they're loyal. And just because someone says they've worked with foreign investors doesn't mean they served them well. In fact, some specifically target foreign investors because they perceive them as easier to exploit due to distance and lack of local knowledge.

Always ask for references and actually call them, asking probing questions about their experience. Request proof of past work; for contractors, ask for addresses of completed projects you can verify, and for property managers, ask for sample reports or redacted lease agreements. Always insist on formal, legally binding written agreements (contracts) for every service. Define clear expectations for responsiveness, reporting frequency, and preferred communication channels.

And make sure your team works for YOU—not for each other, and certainly not for the seller who referred them. Because in this industry, especially in distressed markets, it's not uncommon for the property manager, contractor, and even the seller to be friends, family, or worse, part of a quiet hustle you're the last to find out about. Conflicts of interest are rampant; your job is to identify and avoid them.

Treat Your Team Like an Investment: The Ownership Mentality

Real estate is not a one-person show. It demands a collective effort. But just because you need help doesn't mean you should settle for just "bodies that breathe." You don't build lasting wealth with warm bodies who merely perform tasks. You build wealth with aligned, accountable professionals who share your vision.

Hire with proof, not personality. Don't hire someone just because they sound confident, charismatic, or have a smooth sales pitch. Hire because they show verifiable proof of competence, integrity, and a track record of consistent results. This means asking them to show you the leases they currently manage and how they handle tenant issues, or to show you the last five renovations they completed, with before-and-after photos and final budgets. Demand to see their license, their insurance, their timeline for the project, and their books or reporting samples, not just their word. We don't hire based on hope. We hire based on history, verifiable performance, and a clear commitment to transparency.

Loyalty isn't enough; the vision comes first. Don't keep someone just because they've been "with you from the beginning" or because you feel a sense of personal loyalty. This isn't a friendship circle—it's an investment company. Your loyalty belongs to your investment vision, your protection, and your financial goals. They've disqualified themselves if they haven't grown as your business has grown, becoming more sophisticated in their reporting or service, or if they resist structure, transparency, or accountability. They are also problematic if they consistently disappear when it matters most, leaving you in the dark, or if they cut corners, perform shoddy work, or expect you not to notice. Ultimately, if they are costing you money through negligence or incompetence, you can be grateful for their past help, acknowledge their efforts, and still replace them. Because your loyalty belongs to the vision—not the vendor. Your investment's success must always take precedence over personal comfort or misplaced loyalty.

What you're really looking for is ownership mentality. This is the key differentiator in a truly effective support team: You don't just want helpers or order-takers. You want partners who move like they've got equity in the outcome—even if they don't. That's called ownership mentality. It's the property manager who doesn't wait for you to chase them for updates—they proactively update you weekly, anticipating your questions. It's the contractor who double-checks city codes and permit requirements before you even ask, ensuring compliance. It's the CPA who reminds you of filing deadlines and new tax strategies because they're thinking long game, not just annual returns. It's the field representative who walks your property like it's their own name on the deed, noticing every detail and proactively addressing potential issues. It's the attorney who not only reviews contracts but also advises on potential future legal risks. Those are the people you keep. Ownership mentality isn't about ego—it's about stewardship. It's about professionals who carry the weight of your investment with you, who understand that your win is their win, and your loss is their problem too. They are invested in your success, not just their fee.

You don't need a team that works for you. You need a team that works with you. And the only way to get that is to vet deeply, going beyond the surface, beyond the referrals, and beyond the sales pitch. Set clear expectations by defining roles, responsibilities, communication protocols, and performance metrics in writing. Document agreements by ensuring every relationship is governed by a clear, legally binding contract. Hold people accountable by regularly reviewing performance against expectations and addressing shortcomings promptly. And replace quickly when standards aren't met; don't let underperformers jeopardize your investment.

Because hope is not a management strategy. And comfort is not the same as competency. Your support system is your ultimate leverage as an international investor. Build it wisely, nurture it diligently, and it will serve as the engine that drives your Strategy forward and protects your Structure for years to come.

Reflection Check-In:

Before You Scale Another Door—Audit Your Team

This isn't about sounding smart on a Zoom call. This is about real protection, real partnership, and real power. Because one weak link on your team can cost you more than a bad deal ever could.

First, identify who's actually on your team right now—and have you truly vetted each one? Make a list. Write down the name and role of every person involved in your U.S. real estate business right now: Your property manager, your real estate agent, your contractor, your CPA, your attorney, your bookkeeper, your insurance broker, your local field partner or trusted advisor. Now, for each one, ask yourself: Did I vet them independently—or did someone else recommend them, and I just ran with it? Do I have signed, detailed agreements with clear expectations in writing for their role? Have I recently reviewed their work, asked for proof of performance, or checked for gaps in their service? If you wouldn't trust them with your bank password, why are you trusting them with your property, your income, and your legal liability?

Next, consider where there are gaps in your support system right now. Be honest. Are you depending too heavily on one person to wear too many hats (e.g., a property manager who also acts as your sole contractor and financial advisor)? Do you have someone local to walk your properties independently and verify what you're being told by others? Do you have an attorney and CPA who truly understand U.S. real estate and foreign investor nuances? Do you have a real system for documentation, or are you still "winging it" through email threads and verbal agreements? Remember—vulnerability doesn't always look like disaster. It often hides in the places you've been "meaning to fix" or in the assumptions you've made.

Finally, if something went wrong tomorrow, who would you call—and do you fully trust them to handle it? Imagine a crisis: If your property flooded due to a burst pipe, if your tenant stopped paying rent and refused to leave, if the city sent a major code violation notice, if a buyer backed out at the last second on a sale, or if a contractor walked off the job halfway through a renovation. Who's on speed dial? More importantly—do you trust them implicitly to handle it competently, transparently, and without costing you more than necessary? Do they move like owners, taking proactive responsibility, or merely like order-takers, waiting for your instruction? Do they keep you informed—or keep you chasing them for answers? If the answer to any of these questions makes you uncomfortable, good. Because that discomfort is precisely what prevents disaster. Your real estate business is only as strong as the people running it with you. And if you don't trust your team, you don't have one.

Chapter 6: Due Diligence

The Art of Verification Before You Buy

Trust, but verify.

We've meticulously built the foundational pillars of your investor readiness. In "The Awakening," you embraced a strategic mindset. In "Strategy," you crafted your personalized blueprint, defining your investment identity and micro-market focus. In "Structure," you learned to shield your assets with robust legal and financial frameworks. And in "Support," you understood the critical importance of a meticulously vetted, on-the-ground team.

Now, it's time to apply these pillars directly to the most critical phase of any investment: **Due Diligence**. This chapter isn't about cleaning up messes—it's about proactively preventing them. It's about transforming from a hopeful buyer into a discerning, empowered investor who verifies every claim, scrutinizes every detail, and understands the true nature of an asset before a single dollar is wired. The tool that separates a smart investor from a desperate, miseducated buyer is rigorous, uncompromising due diligence.

Due Diligence Is Not Just a Step—
It's a Skillset and a Mindset

Let's break the fantasy that due diligence is a mere checklist item, something to be outsourced and forgotten. It is far more profound. You are not buying a spreadsheet, a glossy photo, or a smooth sales pitch. You are buying a physical address with a complex history, a specific reputation within its community, and inherent, often hidden, risks. And if you don't know how to forensically investigate that address—its past, its present, and its true potential—before you wire your hard-earned money, you're not investing; you're gambling with your future.

Due diligence is not a suggestion. It's your absolute, non-negotiable insurance policy that you purchase with time, effort, and critical thinking *before* you ever touch the closing table. It's the meticulous process of verifying every claim, uncovering every hidden liability, and confirming every assumption. It is the active application of your **Strategy** (knowing what to look for based on your plan), your **Structure** (having the legal framework to conduct proper checks), and your **Support** system (the trusted individuals who execute the verification on the ground).

The Truth? Most Foreign Investors Skip This Entirely

It's a harsh reality, but a common one. Why do most international investors, intelligent and often successful in their own fields, bypass this absolutely critical phase of due diligence? Fundamentally, it comes down to a lack of knowledge and miseducation, as no one taught them how to verify. The "turnkey" model, in particular, actively discourages independent due diligence, promising to handle "everything" for you. Investors are led to believe that a quick glance at a pro forma and a few photos are sufficient, and they don't know what questions to ask, what documents to demand, or what public records exist.

Another reason is a blind trust in the seller or wholesaler. They assume the agent, wholesaler, or "investment company" is telling the whole truth, that their interests are aligned. They fail to recognize the inherent conflict of interest when the seller is also the source of all information and recommendations. Compounding this is a perceived distance barrier; being thousands of miles away, many investors mistakenly believe "there's nothing I can do from here" to conduct thorough checks. This feeling of helplessness is precisely what bad actors exploit, leveraging your geographical distance as their strategic advantage.

Furthermore, the fear of losing the deal plays a significant role. High-pressure sales tactics, like "Act now or lose this amazing deal!", create a fear of missing out (FOMO). Investors rush, skipping vital steps, because they're afraid the "opportunity" will vanish, prioritizing speed over safety. Lastly, the desire for "passive" income drives them. The dream of effortless wealth leads them to delegate blindly, assuming that once they hand over the money, all problems disappear, and they don't want to engage in the "dirty work" of due diligence.

But here's the reality: You don't need to live in the U.S. to perform effective due diligence. In fact, many investors who do live here still fail to do their homework thoroughly. You're certainly not alone in facing this challenge. (Perhaps I should write a book for my novice U.S. investors too, but I digress!) The crucial takeaway is that geographic distance doesn't excuse, nor does it prevent, meticulous verification. You just need the right Strategy (knowing what questions to ask), the right Structure (the legal entity and banking to handle transactions transparently), the right Support system (your trusted eyes and ears on the ground), and crucially, the right mindset—one of proactive verification and healthy skepticism.

What Smart Due Diligence Actually Looks Like: A Forensic Approach

Before you buy anything, before you sign a purchase agreement, you (or, more realistically and effectively, your meticulously vetted Support System acting on your behalf) should verify every single one of these critical elements. This is your forensic investigation into the property's past, present, and true future potential.

Your first step is obtaining a **Title Report: Unmasking Ownership and Hidden Claims**. This is a comprehensive report from a title company that examines public records to confirm the legal ownership of the property and identify any encumbrances, liens, or claims against it. It's crucial because it's your primary defense against buying someone else's debt or legal problem. This report will reveal if there are liens or judgments, such as unpaid contractor bills, old mortgages, IRS tax liens, child support judgments, or even old utility bills, all of which can attach to the property and become your responsibility after closing. It also uncovers unpaid taxes or city violations, which can accrue and become a lien, potentially leading to foreclosure if not paid. Crucially, it verifies that the seller is legally allowed to sell the property, confirming that the person or entity selling the property is the true legal owner and has the authority to convey title, protecting against fraudulent sales. Finally, it ensures the title company guarantees clear ownership by issuing title insurance, which protects you (the buyer) and your lender against future claims against the property's title. To verify this, your U.S. real estate attorney or title company (part of your Support System) will order and meticulously review the title report, identifying any clouds on title and ensuring they are cleared before closing. A critical rule is to always use a qualified real estate attorney or title company for title examination and deed transfers, never "Quit Claim" the deed yourself or accept one from an individual, as this offers virtually no protection against hidden title issues. When wiring funds safely, always wire money directly to your trusted U.S. real estate attorney or title company. Never, under any circumstances, wire money to an individual, even if they claim to be involved in the transaction, as wire fraud is rampant, and scammers often impersonate real estate agents, sellers, or even attorneys via email to trick you into sending funds to fraudulent accounts. Always independently verify wiring instructions by calling your attorney or title company using a phone number you know to be legitimate (e.g., from their official website, not an email signature).

Next is **Tenant Verification: Confirming Income and Occupancy**. This is the process of verifying the existence of tenants, their payment history, and the validity of their lease agreements. It's crucial because the "phantom tenant" scam is rampant; you need to know if the property is truly occupied, if the tenants are paying, and if their lease terms align with the seller's claims. To verify, demand a current rent roll, which is a detailed list of all tenants, their unit numbers, monthly rent, move-in dates, and payment history for at least the last 6-12 months. Request copies of all executed leases and review these with your attorney, looking for lease terms, rent amounts, security deposit details, and any special clauses. Verify security deposits, confirming the amount held and how they will be transferred to you at closing. Direct tenant contact (with property manager assistance) is vital; have your property manager or trusted local advisor attempt to contact the tenants (with proper notice) to confirm their occupancy and satisfaction, as this is crucial for verifying the human element. Most sellers will say they don't want the tenant to know they are selling, which could be a red flag, because if a tenant is happy with where they live, they will want to stay. Also, request recent utility bills (water, gas, electric) to confirm active usage, which indicates occupancy.

Following that is **Lead Paint Registry and Environmental Hazards: Protecting Health and Avoiding Lawsuits**. This involves researching if the property has been flagged for lead-based paint hazards, especially if built before 1978, and checking for other environmental concerns like asbestos, mold, or underground storage tanks. This is crucial because lead paint can cause severe health problems, particularly in children, leading to devastating lawsuits and mandatory, expensive abatement costs, making ignoring this a massive liability. To verify, federal law mandates that sellers of homes built before 1978 disclose any known lead-based paint hazards, so you should always demand this disclosure, and it's a good practice to assume lead paint is present if the house was built before 1978. Homes from that era, particularly those constructed before the 1960s, have a higher likelihood of containing lead-based paint. Many cities and counties maintain a lead registry or database of properties with known lead hazards or abatement orders, so have your local Support System check this. If there's any doubt about lead-based paint, or if you plan to renovate, it's highly advisable to hire a certified lead-based paint inspector to test the property. Crucially, be aware that some cities, like Cleveland and Detroit, have mandatory lead-safe inspection requirements that properties must pass to be rented legally. Even minor issues like chipped paint can trigger requirements to repaint both interior and exterior surfaces to meet these standards. Having a thorough inspection done during your due diligence period can save you thousands of dollars and significant headaches later on, by catching these potential issues before you close. For older or industrial properties, consider a Phase I Environmental Site Assessment (ESA) to identify potential contamination.

Another vital check is **Code Violations and City Orders: Legal Rentability and Hidden Fines**. This involves checking for any outstanding code violations, nuisance orders, demolition orders, or other legal issues issued by the city or county against the property. It's crucial because a property with active code violations might not be legally rentable, can accrue daily fines, and could even be condemned by the city, rendering your investment worthless. To verify, have your local Support System (or your attorney) directly contact the city's building department or code enforcement office for the specific property address and request a full report of all open and closed violations. In many cities, rental properties must be registered and undergo periodic inspections to obtain a Certificate of Occupancy

(CO) or rental permit, so verify that the property has a valid, current rental registration and CO, and that it hasn't been revoked. Also, check demolition lists, as some cities maintain public lists of properties slated for demolition due to severe blight or structural issues.

Then comes **Rehab Verification: Quality of Work and Hidden Flaws**. This means assessing the quality and completeness of any renovations claimed by the seller and identifying if permits were pulled for major work. This is crucial because the "bait-and-switch" rehab is common, where superficial cosmetic work can hide major structural, plumbing, electrical, or roofing issues that will become your expensive problem. To verify, get an independent home inspection from a licensed home inspector who will identify general condition issues, including signs of shoddy rehab work. For older homes or properties with visible issues, consider specialized inspections for roof, HVAC, plumbing, electrical, and foundation. Check the city's building department for records of permits pulled for any major renovations; if significant work was done without permits, it's a huge red flag and could lead to fines or forced re-work. Finally, if the seller used a specific contractor, research that contractor's reputation and licensing.

Next, you need **Neighborhood Intelligence: The Lived Reality of the Block**. This is about going beyond statistics to understand the qualitative aspects of the immediate block and surrounding micro-market. It's crucial because statistics can be misleading, and you need to know the true feel and trajectory of the specific street your property is on. To verify, have your local real estate agent or trusted advisor conduct a detailed video walkthrough of the exact block at different times of day (e.g., 9 AM and 9 PM). Ask them to point out the number of boarded-up homes or vacant lots, signs of illegal dumping or loitering, the general upkeep of neighboring properties, the presence of active community members or neighborhood watch signs, and proximity to any undesirable elements (e.g., abandoned buildings, high-traffic liquor stores). Ask your agent for recent sales activity (comps) on that exact block for the last 6-12 months, as this shows how quickly properties are selling and at what price point. Also, look for signs of community engagement: Are there active neighborhood associations? Community gardens? Local businesses that seem to be thriving? These are signs of a healthy, engaged community.

Another essential element is **Zoning and Usage: Legal Compliance for Your Strategy**. This involves verifying that the property's zoning allows for your intended use (e.g., single-family rental, multi-family, short-term rental). It's crucial because operating a property outside its legal zoning can lead to massive fines, forced changes in use, or even demolition orders. To verify, have your attorney or local Support System verify the property's zoning designation with the City Planning/Zoning Department and ensure it aligns with your investment strategy (e.g., if you plan to convert a single-family to a duplex, is that allowed?). Check for specific usage restrictions, such as local ordinances against short-term rentals (like Airbnb bans), restrictions on the number of unrelated tenants, or specific requirements for Section 8 approval. Also, research any planned city developments (e.g., new roads, commercial zones, public transit lines) nearby that could impact property value, desirability, or even lead to eminent domain.

Finally, obtain **Insurance Quotes: Feasibility and Cost of Protection**. This involves obtaining actual insurance quotes for a landlord policy and umbrella coverage before you buy. It's crucial because some properties in high-risk areas may be uninsurable, or the premiums might be so high that they kill your cash flow projections. To verify, work with a U.S. insurance broker who specializes in rental properties and understands inner-city risks, providing them with the exact address and property details. Get multiple quotes from different carriers to ensure competitive pricing and comprehensive coverage. Have the broker clearly explain what the policy doesn't cover (e.g., flood, mold, specific types of vandalism).

Case Study: The Hidden Costs of Skipping Due Diligence – The Property That Was Already Condemned

Let's talk about a client of mine from France, a highly successful entrepreneur in his home country. He was drawn to the U.S. market by the promise of affordable properties and high cash flow, particularly in Cleveland. He bought what he believed was a solid, cash-flowing duplex on the east side of Cleveland. The photos looked good, the price was incredibly low, and the pitch from the "turnkey" provider was smooth: "fully renovated, tenant in place, and ready to go." He was assured it was a truly passive investment.

What he didn't know, and what the seller conveniently "forgot" to disclose, was that the property was already on the city's condemnation list—meaning it had been legally flagged as unsafe for human occupancy and was slated for potential demolition. It wasn't rent-ready. It wasn't livable. And legally, it shouldn't have even been sold without full, explicit disclosure of its condemned status.

Here's the kicker, and the devastating lesson in due diligence: All of that critical information—the condemnation order, the structural violations, the revoked occupancy permit—was public record. It was available at the city's building department, the housing court, and the code enforcement office. Had he, or his Support System, simply called the city's building department or housing court for that specific address, he would've learned the home was cited for major structural violations, including a crumbling foundation and a compromised roof. Had he pulled the code enforcement report, he would've seen that the city was actively preparing to pursue demolition due to the severity of the issues. Had he asked for proof of current rental registration or a valid certificate of occupancy, he would've discovered it had been revoked months prior, making it illegal to rent.

But no one told him. And he didn't know to check. He relied on the seller's assurances and the curated photos. So, he wired the money.

And bought a property that couldn't legally house a tenant, couldn't generate income, and was a ticking time bomb of fines and potential demolition, leading to demolition costs, no rent, no recourse, just profound regret, immense financial loss, and the emotional toll of being utterly exploited.

The Lesson? Due diligence isn't paranoia. It's protection. And in cities like Cleveland, Baltimore, Detroit, or Memphis—where code violations are common, property conditions vary wildly, and oversight can be weak—it's entirely up to you to verify before you invest. Because once the deal is closed, the problem becomes yours, and yours alone.

Due Diligence Is a Filter—Use It Ruthlessly

When you implement due diligence correctly, methodically, and without compromise, bad deals don't just become apparent—they disqualify themselves. The process acts as a ruthless filter, separating the legitimate opportunities from the deceptive traps.

The house might be incredibly cheap… The projected rent might be high on paper… The pitch might sound smooth and irresistible…

But when you truly dig in, when you apply your strategic filters and leverage your support system for independent verification, the truth shows up. You discover that the ROI is fake, based on inflated income or underestimated expenses. The rehab is dirty, a cosmetic cover-up hiding major structural or system failures. The management is shady, with a history of non-transparency or outright fraud. The tenant has no valid lease, or a history of non-payment. The property is a lawsuit waiting to happen, with undisclosed hazards or code violations. And the neighborhood is declining, despite what the "revitalization" narrative suggests.

And then? You walk away empowered—not because you couldn't buy it, but because you knew better. You chose not to buy it. This is the power of discernment.

This Is Where Real Investors Win: The Power of No

Real investors don't win because they bought the cheapest deal. They win because they didn't buy the wrong one. Their success is as much about the deals they avoid as it is about the deals they acquire.

Due diligence isn't about killing momentum. It's about preserving your capital, your sanity, and your future opportunities. It ensures that every investment you make is a calculated, informed decision, not a desperate gamble. You can still move fast in a competitive market—but you have to move informed, with precision and confidence, knowing that your verification process has protected you.

This commitment to rigorous due diligence is the ultimate expression of your Investor Readiness. It demonstrates that you have fully embraced your Strategy, fortified your Structure, and built an indispensable Support system. It is the culmination of your re-education, transforming you into a formidable player in the unseen game.

Reflection Check-In:

Before You Send a Wire, Ask Yourself This...

What steps do I currently take before sending a wire for a property—and where am I still guessing or relying on others' assurances? Do you pause to independently verify city records, including permits, code violations, and tax status? Do you pull title reports yourself (or have your attorney do it) and meticulously review them—or do you just assume the seller's paperwork is clean? Have you seen verifiable proof of current rent, valid lease terms, and actual occupancy? Are you trusting that the rehab was genuinely done because someone said "it's turnkey" or provided a few photos, without independent verification? If you're relying on gut feelings, secondhand promises, or convenience—you're gambling, not investing. So, be honest: Where are you truly informed—and where are you just guessing?

Do I have a standardized, comprehensive due diligence checklist, or am I relying on what others tell me? Real investors don't move off memory or casual conversations. They move off a defined process. Do you have your own detailed due diligence checklist that you follow for every single property, regardless of how good it looks? Or are you just trusting the documents others send you, without independent verification? If your entire analysis and decision-making process is built solely on what a wholesaler, property manager, or seller says… you're not protecting yourself. You're positioning yourself to be taken advantage of. Information that isn't independently verified isn't valuable; it's a liability.

Am I afraid to dig deeper because I don't want to "lose" the deal? Be brutally honest with yourself. Have you ever skipped a crucial due diligence step because you didn't want to "offend" the seller or broker? Or because you feared the deal would go to someone else if you took too long? This fear is precisely what bad actors' prey upon. The best deals are those that stand up to rigorous scrutiny. If a deal can't withstand thorough due diligence, it wasn't a good deal to begin with. Your willingness to walk away from a bad deal, even a seemingly attractive one, is the ultimate sign of your readiness and discipline as an investor.

Chapter 7: The Unseen Game

Proactive Defense Against Deception

You can't win a game you don't even know you're playing.

We've meticulously built the foundational pillars of your investor readiness. In "The Awakening," you embraced a strategic mindset, moving beyond passive hope to active discernment. In "Strategy," you crafted your personalized blueprint, defining your investment identity and micro-market focus with precision. In "Structure," you learned to shield your assets with robust legal and financial frameworks, transforming properties into protected business operations. And in "Support," you understood the critical importance of a meticulously vetted, on-the-ground team—your eyes, ears, and hands—to bridge the inherent distance of overseas investing. Most recently, in "Due Diligence," you mastered the forensic approach to scrutinizing every detail of a potential investment.

Now, it's time to pull all these interconnected pillars together. This chapter is about equipping you with the ultimate discernment to play **"The Unseen Game"**—the subtle, often invisible, but pervasive battle against misinformation, manipulation, and outright fraud that permeates the landscape of distressed U.S. real estate. You've learned the principles; now we apply them to proactively spot the scams, avoid the pitfalls, and truly see the game before you get played by it. You are no longer merely miseducated; you are becoming ready to see the invisible, understand the unspoken rules, and act as your own most formidable defense.

The Landscape of Deception: Why It's So Easy to Get Played

The U.S. inner-city real estate market, particularly in cities like Cleveland, Detroit, Memphis, Baltimore, and St. Louis, presents a unique and compelling paradox. On one hand, it genuinely offers significant opportunities for substantial returns, often at lower entry costs than more established markets, and the chance to make a positive community impact. On the other, it's very characteristics—the allure of low property values, high demand for affordable housing, and a perceived lack of local oversight for distant investors—make it an incredibly fertile ground for deception, misrepresentation, and outright fraud.

This fertile ground for exploitation is cultivated by several insidious factors, each contributing to the vulnerability of the distant, miseducated investor. First, **Information Asymmetry: The Knowledge Gap as a Weapon**. You, the international investor, are thousands of miles away, relying almost entirely on information provided by others. The sellers, wholesalers, "turnkey" companies, and even some unscrupulous property managers possess all the local, on-the-ground knowledge, and they meticulously control the flow of information to you. They know precisely which properties have hidden code violations, which blocks struggle with rampant crime, which "renovations" are merely cosmetic cover-ups, and which tenants are chronic non-payers. This fundamental imbalance of information is not just a disadvantage; it is a ripe opportunity for exploitation. They feed you what they want you to see, not the full, unvarnished truth, carefully curating a narrative that serves their interests, not yours. Your distance becomes their strategic advantage.

Another powerful factor is **The "Easy Money" Narrative: The Siren Song of Effortless Wealth**. The promise of high, passive returns with minimal effort is incredibly seductive. It taps into a universal human desire for financial freedom and can powerfully override common sense, critical thinking, and the necessity for rigorous due diligence. In a world constantly seeking shortcuts to wealth, the idea of buying a property in America, having someone else manage it effortlessly, and watching money flow into your bank account is a powerful, almost hypnotic, lure. This narrative actively encourages investors to bypass the hard work of understanding the market, vetting their partners, and building a robust operational structure, leading them straight into the arms of those who profit directly from their naiveté and desire for a quick, uncomplicated win.

Then there's the **Lack of Uniform Regulation and Enforcement: Pockets of the Wild West**. While real estate transactions are indeed regulated in the U.S., the nuances of state and local laws, licensing requirements for various professionals (especially for wholesalers and property managers, which can vary wildly by state and even city), and the actual enforcement of these regulations differ dramatically. What's perfectly legal or loosely enforced in one state or county might be a major red flag or outright illegal in another. This patchwork of inconsistent regulations creates loopholes that bad actors ruthlessly exploit, operating in jurisdictions where oversight is minimal, and penalties for misconduct are rare or difficult to impose. Foreign investors, unfamiliar with these intricate local variations, are often left bewildered, unprotected, and without clear recourse when things go wrong.

The **"American Dream" Mystique: Blind Trust in a Brand** also plays a significant role. For many foreign investors, the U.S. represents a beacon of stability, boundless opportunity, and a strong, trustworthy legal system. This perception, while generally true at a macro level, can lead to a dangerous and often fatal assumption that all U.S. real estate transactions are inherently safe, transparent, and ethical, regardless of the specific parties involved or the particular market segment. They assume the "American brand" of business means automatic integrity, failing to realize that even within a robust legal system, predatory individuals and companies can and do operate. This blind, uncritical trust makes them less likely to question, less likely to verify, and far more susceptible to polished presentations and deceptive promises.

Finally, consider the **High Volume, Low Quality: The Needle in the Haystack (of Problems)**. In some distressed markets, the sheer volume of cheap, often dilapidated properties means there's a constant churn of transactions. This high volume makes it easier for bad actors to operate under the radar, moving from one fraudulent deal to the next. One victim's realization that they've been scammed is quickly followed by the perpetrators moving on to new targets or dissolving their entities, making recovery of funds incredibly difficult. The focus shifts from quality and integrity to rapid turnover and minimal accountability, making it exceptionally challenging for an outsider to discern legitimate, viable opportunities from outright scams or deeply problematic assets.

These factors combine to create a perfect storm where the miseducated investor, lacking a robust Strategy (to identify genuine opportunity), a protective Structure (to shield their assets and ensure compliance), and a reliable Support system (to provide independent oversight and local intelligence), becomes the perfect target for exploitation. They are the unwitting participants in an "unseen game" where the rules are rigged against them from the start, and the consequences are often devastating. You can't win a game you don't even know you're playing.

Common Scam Tactics Revisited: How They Exploit Your Blind Spots

Let's revisit some of the common tactics we've touched upon in previous chapters and explicitly link them to how they exploit your lack of Strategy, Structure, and Support. Understanding how these scams work, and the psychological levers they pull, is your first and most crucial line of defense. This is where your re-education truly pays dividends.

1. The "Sight Unseen" Sell (Exploiting Lack of Strategy & Support)

This is the foundational deception. Sellers, wholesalers, or "turnkey" companies aggressively push you to buy properties without ever physically seeing them. They rely heavily on glossy, professional-looking photos (often outdated, digitally enhanced, or even from different properties), carefully edited virtual tours (that strategically avoid problem areas), and inflated proformas. The sales pitch is often laced with urgency: "It's a hot market, you need to act fast before it's gone!" or "We handle everything, no need for you to travel, it's truly passive!" They cunningly frame your geographical distance as a benefit, not a profound risk. Your physical distance creates a profound inability to verify the property's true current condition, the actual state of the neighborhood (beyond a static Google Street View image), or the real quality of any purported "rehab." You are forced to trust pixels and smooth talk over tangible reality. You're buying a concept, a promise, not a concrete asset, and that concept is often a mirage.

The S3 framework — Strategy, Structure, and Support — is your ultimate defense against the "Unseen Game" of misinformation and hidden risks. When applied to due diligence, each pillar plays a vital, interconnected role in safeguarding your investment. Your **Investment Strategy** must dictate that you have a clear, verifiable understanding of the property's actual condition and its precise market context. This means adopting a non-negotiable rule: no independent, on-the-ground physical verification before funds are committed, no deal. Your strategy acts as a powerful filter, ensuring you never move forward based solely on photos or descriptions provided by the seller or their agents. It's about having a strategic firewall that prevents you from buying sight unseen or without crucial independent confirmation. Your **Support** system, a trusted advisor or independent, licensed property inspector on the ground, is absolutely essential. This person acts as your literal eyes and ears, physically verifying the property's condition, taking current, unedited, comprehensive photos and videos, and critically assessing the immediate surroundings, including the block's overall appearance, occupancy rates, and any visible signs of distress (e.g., abandoned cars, excessive litter, signs of vandalism). This proxy ensures you're not buying a phantom, a money pit, or a property in a rapidly declining area.

2. The "Ghost Manager" or "Phantom Tenant" (Exploiting Lack of Structure & Support)

With this tactic, you're told the property is "fully tenanted" or "under professional management," and for a short period, you might even receive rent payments (which could be fronted by the scammer). But then the manager becomes unresponsive, the rent stops arriving, or you discover the "tenant" is either non-existent, a relative of the scammer placed temporarily, or a problem tenant whose issues were deliberately concealed. They might send fake rent rolls, doctored financial statements, or simply stop communicating altogether after your funds are secured. Your inability to independently verify the tenant's actual existence, their legitimate payment history, or the property manager's true performance and accountability becomes your blind spot. You're relying entirely on their word and their doctored paperwork, without any independent checks.

A robust **legal structure** includes clear, legally binding property management agreements drafted by your U.S. attorney, with predefined Key Performance Indicators (KPIs), strict reporting requirements (e.g., monthly statements with supporting invoices), and explicit consequences for non-performance or breach of contract. It also involves establishing separate, dedicated U.S. business bank accounts (as discussed in Chapter 4) to track funds transparently, making it far harder for managers to commingle or misappropriate funds without detection. Your **Support** system, through a trusted advisor or independent oversight (beyond the property manager), should conduct periodic, unannounced property checks. They should verify tenant occupancy (e.g., by checking utility bills in the tenant's name, or discreetly confirming with neighbors). They must meticulously audit financial reports against actual invoices and bank statements, looking for discrepancies. They can also attempt to contact tenants directly (within ethical boundaries and with proper notice) to confirm their presence, satisfaction, and rent payment status, serving as a crucial verification layer.

3. The "Bait-and-Switch" Rehab (Exploiting Lack of Strategy & Support)

Here, you're promised a full, high-quality renovation that justifies the purchase price and projected rent. However, the contractor does shoddy work, uses inferior materials, cuts corners (e.g., painting over mold, not addressing structural issues, using cheap fixtures), or simply disappears with your money. They might send photos of a different, well-renovated property, or only show pictures of the finished, superficial aspects, carefully hiding the underlying flaws. Your blind spot lies in your inability to physically inspect the quality of the work at various stages of the renovation, verify the materials actually used against the agreed-upon scope, or hold the contractor accountable in person for substandard work or abandonment. You're relying on their integrity, which is often non-existent, and their ability to deceive with carefully selected imagery.

Your **investment strategy** must include a detailed, line-item scope of work for the rehab, milestone-based payments tied to verified completion, and a realistic contingency budget (e.g., 15-20% of the rehab cost) for unforeseen issues. It dictates vetting contractors independently and never paying 100% upfront. Through your **Support** system, a trusted advisor or independent project manager on the ground is absolutely critical for overseeing the rehab. They should conduct regular, documented site visits, verify work quality at each payment milestone, approve invoices only for completed and satisfactory work, and ensure the project stays on track and on budget. They are your quality control and your enforcer, ensuring your investment is protected from shoddy workmanship and outright theft.

4. The "Hidden Liabilities" Property (Exploiting Lack of Structure & Strategy)

With this tactic, you buy a property that has undisclosed liens (e.g., unpaid contractor bills, utility liens, HOA liens), significant back taxes, unaddressed city code violations, severe environmental issues (like lead paint, asbestos, or extensive mold), or major structural defects that were intentionally concealed or simply not disclosed. These issues only emerge after closing, becoming your expensive, unexpected problem. Your blind spot is your lack of comprehensive due diligence beyond what the seller provides, and your unfamiliarity with local regulations, complex public records systems, and the specific disclosure laws (or lack thereof) in that particular state. You're buying a ticking time bomb because you didn't know where to look for the fuse.

Your **legal structure**, meticulously facilitated by a competent U.S. real estate attorney, ensures thorough title searches (to uncover all liens, judgments, and ownership disputes), meticulous review of all available public records, and proper closing procedures to uncover hidden liabilities before you close. They are your legal detective, ensuring you acquire clear title. Your **Strategy** for investment includes a non-negotiable requirement for comprehensive due diligence. This means commissioning professional, independent inspections (general home inspection, structural engineering report if needed, environmental assessments for lead/asbestos/mold), and a meticulous review of all city/county records for permits, code violations, and tax history. This proactive, multi-layered approach uncovers problems before they become your responsibility.

5. The "Too Good to Be True" Numbers (Exploiting Lack of Strategy)

The tactic here involves the pro forma or pitch deck presented by the seller or promoter showing incredibly high cash flow, unrealistically low expenses, and rapid appreciation that seems almost unbelievable. They might use national averages for expenses in a market where local costs are much higher, or project 100% occupancy in a high-vacancy area. They often omit crucial expenses like vacancy, capital expenditures, or even property management fees. Your blind spot is your eagerness for high returns, your unfamiliarity with realistic market numbers, and a lack of understanding of typical operating expenses and vacancy rates in that specific micro-market. You're falling for the illusion of effortless profit, allowing your desire to override your critical judgment.

Your **investment strategy** must include building your own realistic, conservative financial projections. This means stress-testing the numbers, researching actual comparable rental rates and sales prices for the immediate area (not just the broader zip code), and using conservative estimates for vacancy, repairs, and all other operating expenses. It means understanding that legitimate, sustainable returns are often more modest but far more reliable and predictable than the inflated promises of scammers. Your strategy is your financial truth detector, forcing you to confront reality.

Red Flags: Your Personal Scam Radar – The Warning Signals

Beyond specific tactics, there are universal red flags that should immediately trigger your internal alarm system. These are not just minor inconveniences; they are critical signals that one or more of your S3 pillars are being undermined, and that you are entering dangerous territory. Learn to recognize them instantly and act on them without hesitation.

General Red Flags (Apply to all S3 and indicate systemic issues):

Be wary of **high-pressure sales tactics**, such as "Act now or lose this amazing deal!" or "Limited time offer, properties are going fast!" Any pressure to rush your due diligence, bypass standard procedures, or make a quick decision is a massive, unmistakable red flag. Legitimate, truly great opportunities do not vanish in an hour or require you to suspend critical thinking; urgency is often a tactic to mask deception.

Another glaring sign is **resistance to independent verification**. If they discourage you from getting your own independent inspection, talking to past clients (especially international ones), bringing in your own attorney, or performing any independent due diligence, run—do not walk—away. This is the clearest, most undeniable sign they have something significant to hide, and they are actively trying to control the information you receive.

Watch out for **vague or incomplete documentation**. This includes missing invoices, unclear contracts riddled with loopholes, proformas without detailed, itemized breakdowns of income and expenses, or a persistent reluctance to provide specific addresses, tenant names, or contact information. Transparency is the hallmark of integrity; opacity, ambiguity, and missing paperwork are definitive warning signs.

Any **promises of "guaranteed" returns or "no risk"** should immediately raise suspicion. Real estate, like any investment, involves inherent risks. No legitimate investment can guarantee specific returns, especially in dynamic or volatile markets. Anyone promising "guaranteed" profits or "zero risk" is either naive, misinformed, or, more likely, dishonest.

A **"one-stop shop" without independent oversight** is incredibly risky. A company that insists on handling everything (finding the deal, selling it to you, doing the rehab, managing the property, providing all legal/tax advice) without allowing you to bring in your own independent oversight centralizes control, eliminates crucial checks and balances, and makes fraud significantly easier to execute and conceal.

Be wary of **unsolicited offers from unknown sources**. Deals that come to you out of the blue, especially through social media, unsolicited emails, or cold calls, if they seem "too good to be true," often are. Legitimate, high-quality deals are often found through established networks, referrals, or direct outreach to investors who have already demonstrated readiness, not random, mass solicitations.

Finally, **inconsistent or deteriorating communication** is a major red flag. Frequent changes in your primary contact person, consistently unanswered calls or emails, vague or evasive responses, or a general lack of responsiveness after you've expressed interest or, even worse, after you've sent money, signals a fundamental lack of professionalism, accountability, and potentially, a precursor to a disappearing act.

Strategy-Specific Red Flags (Indicating a flawed approach to opportunity):

If the only selling point is how "cheap" the property is, without a detailed discussion of the neighborhood's long-term trajectory, the quality of the tenant pool, or a viable long-term vision for the asset, this is a **focus solely on price**. Cheap is not always good value; it can often be a trap. Beware of **inflated rent projections**, where rents are significantly higher than verifiable comparable properties in the immediate vicinity, or projections that don't align with the actual condition and amenities of the property. Similarly, **ignoring vacancy rates** in projections, by assuming 100% occupancy without a realistic vacancy buffer (which can be 10-20% in some inner-city markets), is highly unrealistic. If there's **no clear exit plan discussed**, and the seller or advisor cannot articulate how you would realistically sell the property if needed, what its resale value drivers are, or what alternative strategies exist beyond initial cash flow, this is a warning sign. Lastly, **generic market talk**, where they discuss "Cleveland" or "Detroit" as a single, monolithic entity, without acknowledging the vast, block-by-block differences between neighborhoods, their unique challenges, and their specific growth patterns, indicates a lack of true market understanding.

Structure-Specific Red Flags (Indicating vulnerability and lack of protection):

A strong, immediate indicator that they either don't understand or don't care about your personal liability protection is **advice to buy in personal name**. This is a fundamental and dangerous error. If they tell you an independent U.S. attorney or tax professional isn't necessary, or that their "in-house" legal/tax team is sufficient for your complex international situation, this is **discouraging legal or tax counsel**, a direct threat to your structural integrity and a clear attempt to control information. A significant red flag is **no separate business bank account**, if they propose commingling your funds with theirs, or managing them through their own general operating account, rather than establishing a dedicated U.S. business bank account for your entity. This separation of funds is critical for legal protection and financial transparency. Finally, if they dismiss U.S. tax implications for foreign investors as "simple" or "not a big deal" without referring you to a specialist who can provide detailed, personalized guidance, this is **vague or dismissive tax advice**.

Support-Specific Red Flags (Indicating unreliable partners):

Beware of a **property manager with no verifiable local office or staff**, or an office that looks like a virtual front, or a P.O. box. A legitimate, professional property management company has a physical presence, a team, and a track record. Look out for **no clear reporting schedule or inconsistent reports**, or reports that are consistently late, vague, lack supporting documentation (like invoices), or are difficult to understand. **High property management fees for minimal service**, or hidden fees that aren't clearly outlined in your contract, should be a concern. While respecting tenant privacy, a legitimate manager should have a transparent process for you to verify tenancy if needed or provide anonymized data; complete refusal is suspicious and indicates **reluctance to provide tenant contact info**. A **contractor demanding large upfront payments**, especially without a detailed scope of work, a clear payment schedule tied to milestones, or a willingness to provide lien waivers, is a red flag. Lastly, if you find **team members who are all connected to the seller**, where every professional (broker, contractor, manager, attorney) was "referred" by the original deal source, this creates a significant, often insurmountable, conflict of interest, as their loyalty will likely be to the referrer, not to you.

The Power of Independent Verification: Your Proactive Defense

Knowing the red flags is one thing; actively, rigorously, and independently verifying the truth is another. This is where you leverage your emerging understanding of Strategy, Structure, and Support to become your own most formidable defense. This is your active role in the unseen game, transforming you from a potential victim into a discerning, empowered investor.

1. Verify the Property (Leveraging Strategy & Support):

This is non-negotiable. **Hire an independent, licensed property inspector** who works for you, not the seller or their agent. They should provide a comprehensive report detailing the property's condition, major systems (HVAC, plumbing, electrical), roof, foundation, and any safety concerns. Insist on a detailed video walkthrough from the inspector if you cannot be there. Next, **engage a local real estate agent** (who is not connected to the seller or their network) to do a detailed video walkthrough of the property. Crucially, ask them to also walk the immediate surrounding blocks, pointing out things that aren't in the listing photos: vacant homes, signs of blight, neighborhood activity, proximity to amenities or problem areas. This provides invaluable context that photos alone cannot convey. Your **public records research is digital detective work**. Access the County Assessor's Website to review property tax history, current ownership records, and assessed values. Look for discrepancies or unusually low valuations that might indicate underlying issues. Check the City/County Building Department for any open permits, code violations, or demolition orders associated with the property, which can reveal hidden structural problems or pending fines. Your U.S. real estate attorney will order and review a Deed and Title Search to reveal past ownership, liens, easements, and any encumbrances that could affect your ownership. Finally, use **Google Maps & Street View**, but with a critical, updated eye, as images can be outdated. Look for signs of recent changes, abandoned properties, or commercial activity, and cross-reference what you see with your local agent's observations and recent photos.

2. Verify the Numbers (Leveraging Strategy):

Never just accept the seller's proforma. **Build your own proforma**, creating realistic, conservative financial projections. Use realistic estimates for vacancy, repairs, taxes, insurance, and management fees, modeling these conservatively, assuming higher expenses and lower income than the seller's projections. Have your independent real estate agent pull **market comparables (comps)** for recent rental rates and sales prices for the immediate area (within a few blocks), not just the broader zip code or city. Focus on closed sales for accurate valuation. Even if you plan to hire one, **interview multiple property managers** in the target market. This will give you a realistic sense of typical market rents, common operating expenses, their fees, and their approach to tenant screening and maintenance. Their insights can help validate or challenge the seller's projections.

3. Verify Your Team (Leveraging Support & Structure):

Use state licensing boards (e.g., state real estate commissions, bar associations, CPA boards) to perform **license and professional affiliation checks**, verifying that every professional (real estate agent, broker, property manager, attorney, CPA) is currently licensed, in good standing, and has no disciplinary actions against them. As detailed in Chapter 5, go beyond the provided list for **independent reference checks**. Ask for contact information for past clients (especially international ones) and call them, asking specific, probing questions about communication, problem-solving, financial transparency, and responsiveness. Look for patterns of consistency or inconsistency. Ensure all contracts (purchase agreements, property management agreements, contractor agreements) are meticulously reviewed by your independent U.S. attorney for **clear, attorney-reviewed contracts**. These contracts must clearly define roles, responsibilities, fees, payment schedules, performance metrics, and termination clauses; ambiguity in contracts is a breeding ground for disputes and exploitation. For crucial roles like your trusted advisor or property manager, consider conducting **background checks**, especially if they will handle significant funds or have direct access to your properties.

4. Verify Your Structure (Leveraging Structure):

Before you buy, **consult a U.S. attorney specializing in foreign investment** to advise you on the optimal legal entity for your situation. Simultaneously, **engage a U.S. CPA specializing in foreign investment** to advise you on the tax implications of your chosen structure and your ongoing tax obligations. Finally, ensure your Employer Identification Number (EIN) is properly obtained for your U.S. entity, and your dedicated U.S. business bank account is fully set up and operational before any funds are wired for property purchase or operational expenses. This **confirmation of EIN & dedicated banking** and separation of funds is critical for legal protection and financial transparency.

The Mindset Shift: From Trusting to Discerning – Your Ultimate Defense

This chapter isn't just about a checklist of things to do; it's about a fundamental, transformative mindset shift. You are moving from a vulnerable position of passive trust (which was repeatedly exploited) to one of active, informed discernment. This is the core of becoming a truly ready investor.

Instead of assuming transparency or good intentions, **cultivate a mindset of healthy skepticism**. Ask probing, specific questions. Demand documentation. Verify everything and assume nothing. Actively **build and nurture your network of trusted, independent professionals**. Understand that your team is your strength, and their integrity is your ultimate protection. Learn to **identify red flags before they become crises**. Anticipate potential problems and build contingencies into your strategy and structure. Your proactive approach is your most powerful weapon. Finally, **understand that**

true, sustainable opportunity lies in clarity, rigorous due diligence, and realistic expectations, not in inflated promises or speculative gambles. The truth, however uncomfortable, is always your greatest asset.

My own journey into the "turnkey trap" taught me this lesson profoundly. I had the local knowledge, the passion, and the desire to help, but my initial lack of a robust internal **Structure** for vetting incoming properties and the external **Support** of a fully aligned, independent team led me to compromise. I learned that even with the best intentions, the "unseen game" can pull you into its web if you don't have a rigorous system for seeing through the lies and protecting your own integrity. My experience became the ultimate proof that even the "fixer" needs a robust **Strategy, Structure, and Support** to avoid becoming part of the problem and to truly serve others effectively.

This book is your re-education. It's designed to help you unlearn the dangerous assumptions that led so many investors astray and to truly understand the real game of real estate. You are now equipped with the knowledge of **Strategy, Structure, and Support**—what I call **S^3**. You've already seen the chaos, the devastating losses, and the immense emotional toll that arises from not having these fundamental, interconnected pillars in place. Now, you grasp that S3 isn't just a set of buzzwords; it's the very foundation underpinning every truly successful international real estate investment. These pillars are the absolute keys to playing, and ultimately winning, the real game.

Reflection Check-In:

Are You Ready for The Unseen Game?

This check-in is designed to help you assess your readiness to play, and win, this crucial game. It's about cultivating the **discernment** needed to see beyond the surface and protect your investment.

Where is My Discernment Level for This "Unseen Game"?

The biggest risk isn't just external fraud; it's our own susceptibility to it. Ask yourself:

- Am I actively looking for what's *not* being said, or am I only focusing on what's presented?
- Do I have a healthy skepticism about "too good to be true" scenarios, or do I let excitement override caution?
- How quickly do I question inconsistencies, or do I rationalize them away?
- Am I willing to accept that someone might be intentionally misrepresenting information, or do I assume everyone operates with good intentions?
- What are my emotional triggers that might make me vulnerable to manipulation (e.g., fear of missing out, desire for quick profits, eagerness to close)? This reflection isn't about being cynical but about sharpening your awareness to recognize the red flags that less discerning investors miss.

Am I Relying on Assumption or Actively Seeking Truth?

In the "Unseen Game," information is either your shield or your vulnerability. Consider:

- When presented with a property, do I immediately consider potential downsides or hidden problems, or do I only focus on the positives?
- Am I actively seeking out **independent, third-party verification** for *every* piece of critical information (e.g., property condition, occupancy, repair costs, market value), or am I comfortable relying solely on what others tell me?
- Do I have a structured process for dissecting property financials, or do I trust summarized projections?
- What steps do I take to uncover potential neighborhood issues or zoning challenges that might not be obvious? Remember, information you haven't independently verified isn't valuable; it's a liability waiting to surface. Your proactive pursuit of truth is your strongest defense.

Is My S^3 Framework Fully Engaged for Discernment?

This chapter pulls together your **Strategy, Structure, and Support** to tackle the "Unseen Game." Reflect on how well you're integrating these pillars for ultimate protection:

- **Strategy:** Does my investment strategy have a built-in filter for "no independent verification, no deal"? Am I disciplined enough to walk away if my strategic criteria for truth aren't met?
- **Structure:** Is my legal and financial structure robust enough to handle the complexities and potential disputes that arise from misinformation, providing a layer of protection?
- **Support:** Am I leveraging my trusted ground crew (attorneys, inspectors, local advisors) to be my eyes, ears, and truth-seekers, providing objective data against what might be presented to me?

Mindset: Am I cultivating a mindset of **proactive verification and healthy skepticism**, recognizing that this vigilance isn't a roadblock, but the very path to genuine success? When your S3 framework is fully engaged, you're not just playing the game—you're playing to win.

Chapter 8: Building Legacy, Not Just ROI

The InvestorRedi™ Blueprint

Legacy is the ultimate return on investment—it's the mark you leave on others and the foundation you build for generations to come.

We've journeyed through the intricate landscape of deception, navigated the seductive illusions of easy money, and meticulously built the foundational pillars of your investor readiness. In "The Awakening," you embraced a strategic mindset, moving beyond passive hope to active discernment. In "Strategy," you meticulously crafted your personalized blueprint, defining your investment identity and micro-market focus with precision. In "Structure," you learned to shield your assets with robust legal and financial frameworks, transforming properties into protected business operations. In "Support," you understood the critical importance of a meticulously vetted, on-the-ground team—your eyes, ears, and hands—to bridge the inherent distance of overseas investing. And most recently, in "Due Diligence," you mastered the forensic approach to scrutinizing every detail of a potential investment, learning to identify and avoid the traps of "The Unseen Game."

Now, we reach the culmination of our profound journey. This chapter is about consolidating every piece of invaluable knowledge you've gained, every critical insight you've absorbed, and charting your definitive, actionable path forward. It's about moving beyond merely avoiding pitfalls to actively **"Building Legacy, Not Just R.O.I."**—investing the right way, with purpose, integrity, and a profound understanding of the lasting impact you can have. This is where the theoretical knowledge becomes lived practice, where your investment transcends a mere transaction and becomes a force for positive, sustainable change, contributing to both your financial freedom and the well-being of the communities you touch. You are no longer the miseducated investor, vulnerable to every scam and misleading promise. You are now equipped with the profound knowledge, the unwavering clarity, and the comprehensive framework to transform your investment aspirations into a tangible reality rooted in integrity, protection, sustainable growth, and ultimately, a lasting legacy. This is your **InvestorRedi™ blueprint for lasting success**, a testament to your commitment to unlearning the lies and confidently owning the game.

Beyond The Block:
Investing with Integrity, Earning Trust

Remember the old man on the stoop, the woman sweeping her porch, the kids playing basketball? In Chapter 1, I told you, "That's who you're really buying this house from. Not the bank, not the wholesaler. Them. They're the block. And they'll remember how you showed up." This isn't just a poetic notion or a feel-good sentiment; it's a fundamental, often overlooked, and profoundly practical truth of inner-city investing. The block has a long, collective memory, etched into its very fabric. It remembers every interaction, every promise, and every betrayal.

It remembers the slumlords who let properties crumble, fostering crime, despair, and a sense of abandonment. It remembers the absentee owners who collected rent but never invested a dime back into the property or the community, allowing blight to spread like a disease. It remembers the flippers who patched over problems with cheap materials, leaving new tenants with recurring headaches and the neighborhood with another quickly deteriorating asset. It remembers the investors who disappeared the moment things got tough, abandoning properties, leaving a trail of blight, broken promises, and unpaid taxes. These negative memories create deep-seated distrust, making it harder for any new investor, even a well-intentioned one, to gain acceptance.

But crucially, the block also remembers those who showed up with genuine intent, those who invested in more than just bricks and mortar. It remembers the landlords who were responsive, the owners who maintained their properties well, and the investors who contributed positively to the neighborhood's stability and revitalization. These positive memories build goodwill, a form of social capital that is priceless.

Investing with integrity means far more than just following the law; it means embodying a set of principles that benefit all stakeholders. This begins with **respecting the community as a stakeholder**. This is the foundational principle, understanding that you are buying into a living, breathing community, a complex social ecosystem, not just a spreadsheet of numbers or a pin on a map. It means acknowledging the rich history, the enduring struggles, and the profound resilience of the people who call that neighborhood home. It means recognizing that your investment impacts their daily lives—their safety, their quality of life, their sense of pride in their surroundings. Therefore, being a good neighbor, even from afar, is paramount. This respect translates into actions like communicating clearly with local leaders, understanding and respecting local norms and cultural nuances, and being sensitive to the existing social fabric. It means not just extracting value but contributing to it.

Next, it involves **embracing a long-term vision with unwavering commitment**. True legacy building is never about quick flips or speculative, short-term gains. It's about a deep, unwavering, long-term commitment to a property and its community. It's about understanding that real appreciation and sustainable cash flow are built incrementally over years, even decades, through consistent care and strategic investment. This means prioritizing consistent, high-quality maintenance, being genuinely responsive to tenant needs, and actively contributing to the neighborhood's stability and improvement. It's about being a consistent, reliable presence, even if that presence is primarily facilitated through your meticulously vetted local Support System. This long-term perspective allows you to weather economic downturns, make wise decisions that benefit both your portfolio and the community, and ultimately reap the compounding rewards of sustained growth and positive impact.

Finally, integrity demands **practicing radical transparency and unwavering fairness**. This is the bedrock of trust, operating with absolute honesty and clarity in all your dealings—with your tenants, your contractors, your property managers, and local officials. It means setting fair, market-aligned rents that are sustainable for the local demographic. It means ensuring timely and thorough repairs, not just patching problems. It means maintaining clear, consistent, and proactive communication with all parties. It means honoring your commitments, even when it's inconvenient or costly. This builds a reputation that precedes you, opening doors to better opportunities and fostering deep, enduring trust within the community and with your team.

When you invest with integrity, the block notices. The subtle signals of responsible ownership are picked up by the informal network of residents. And when the block trusts you, when they see you as a responsible steward rather than just another exploiter, it can become your greatest, unlisted asset. Neighbors become informal guardians of your property, keeping an eye out for issues, reporting suspicious activity, and even helping with minor concerns. Tenants become long-term residents who take pride in and care for their homes, reducing turnover and maintenance headaches. Local leaders become allies, willing to work with you on community initiatives, expedite permits, or even help resolve minor disputes. This intangible asset—community goodwill—translates directly into lower vacancy rates, fewer maintenance emergencies, reduced vandalism, and a more stable, ultimately more profitable investment over time. It's a return on investment that doesn't show up on a spreadsheet but is profoundly real, compounding over time, and fundamentally sustainable. It's the difference between a fleeting profit and a lasting legacy.

A Story of Success: Investing the Right Way, Building a Blueprint

We've heard plenty of cautionary tales, stories of miseducation and devastating losses. These were necessary to illuminate the pitfalls and underscore the urgent need for a new approach. Now, let me tell you about an investor who, by embracing and meticulously applying the principles of Strategy, Structure, and Support, did it right. Her journey serves as a powerful blueprint for the kind of success that is not only financially rewarding but also deeply fulfilling and truly sustainable.

Let's call her Lena, a sharp, analytical businesswoman from Germany. Lena came to me as a referral, before I had even formalized the InvestorRedi™ framework. She was interested in U.S. real estate, but she was wisely cautious, having heard whispers of the very scams and pitfalls I've described throughout this book. She possessed a strong financial background and a disciplined, methodical approach to business, but frankly lacked the on-the-ground knowledge of U.S. inner cities and the intricate nuances of these specific markets. This profound self-awareness—her willingness to admit what she didn't know—was her first strategic advantage.

Lena's initial Strategy was clear, and crucially, it was her own, meticulously defined and personalized, not something sold to her by a third party. She wanted to invest in long-term rental properties in a stable, yet affordable, market. She wasn't chasing astronomical, unrealistic returns; she sought consistent, predictable cash flow and gradual, sustainable appreciation. Most importantly, she was committed to being a responsible, ethical landlord, even from overseas. She understood that her reputation, and the reputation of her investments, was paramount, and that true success meant more than just a number on a balance sheet.

Her very first step, even before looking at a single property, was to meticulously build her Structure. With my guidance, she engaged a U.S. attorney specializing in foreign investment to set up a Limited Liability Company (LLC) that provided maximum liability protection, clearly separating her personal assets from her business ventures. She then worked closely with a U.S. Certified Public Accountant (CPA) to fully understand all her U.S. tax obligations, ensuring she had a clear, compliant plan for both U.S. income tax (including understanding concepts like FIRPTA for future sales) and her home country's tax implications. She navigated the complex process of opening a dedicated U.S. business bank account for her LLC, ensuring complete financial separation and transparency from day one. This upfront investment in structure—in terms of time, effort, and professional fees—gave her immense peace of mind and immediately established her credibility as a serious, legitimate investor. She understood that this wasn't an expense; it was the non-negotiable foundation of her protection and her ability to operate legitimately and confidently.

Next, she focused intently on building her Support system—a multi-layered network of independent, rigorously vetted professionals in her chosen market, Indianapolis. She explicitly rejected the idea of a single "turnkey" provider who controlled all aspects of the investment. Instead, she built her team piece by piece, ensuring each member was accountable directly to her (or through her trusted advisor). This team included a local, independent real estate agent who was not just a salesperson focused on commissions, but possessed deep knowledge of the micro-markets, not just broad zip codes. This agent provided Lena with detailed video walkthroughs of properties and their immediate surrounding blocks, giving Lena a true, unvarnished sense of the neighborhood's pulse, its challenges, and its genuine potential. They were her eyes on the ground for property acquisition, providing objective, unfiltered information.

She also secured a highly reputable property management company with a proven track record of transparent reporting, rigorous tenant screening, and proactive maintenance. Lena reviewed their contracts with her attorney, established clear communication protocols (e.g., weekly email updates, monthly video calls, immediate alerts for emergencies), and set clear performance metrics for tenant retention and expense management. This company served as her hands on the ground for day-to-day operations, acting as her direct proxy. An independent contractor, meticulously vetted through multiple bids and with a strong local reputation for quality work and adherence to timelines, was another key member. Lena insisted on detailed scopes of work, milestone-based payments tied to verified completion, and had her local agent verify work completion before funds were released, ensuring quality and preventing "ghost rehabs" or shoddy workmanship. Her U.S. attorney and CPA remained on retainer for ongoing advice, compliance, and to review any significant contracts or tax implications, serving as her legal and financial guardians, ensuring she remained compliant and optimized. My own role was as her trusted local advisor, serving as her primary point of contact, coordinating her entire ground team, providing independent oversight, and offering nuanced market intelligence that went beyond raw data. I was her strategic partner, ensuring her strategy was executed faithfully and her structural protections were maintained.

Lena's first property was a duplex in a working-class neighborhood in Indianapolis. It wasn't glamorous or in a rapidly gentrifying area, but it was solid, structurally sound, and offered a realistic path to consistent cash flow. Her Strategy for acquisition was to buy at a fair price, perform necessary but not extravagant renovations to ensure safety, habitability, and long-term durability, and target market-rate tenants who valued a well-maintained home and a stable environment. Her Support team ensured the rehab was done right, on budget, and that tenants were thoroughly screened, leading to stable occupancy and reduced turnover.

What truly set Lena apart, however, was her unwavering commitment to the "Beyond the Block" movement—an intentional push to invest ethically, build trust, and leave lasting impact. She instructed her property manager to be highly responsive to tenant needs, to keep the property impeccably well-maintained, and to engage positively and respectfully with the neighbors. When a large, old tree in her yard needed trimming, she didn't just pay for its removal; she offered to have the branches chipped and left for neighbors to use as mulch for their gardens, fostering goodwill. When a tenant had a minor issue, it was addressed promptly, often within hours, demonstrating care and reliability. Her property manager became a familiar, positive presence on the street, known for being fair, responsive, and a good steward.

Over three years, Lena's properties have consistently performed beyond her initial projections. Her vacancy rates are remarkably low, her tenants are long-term and responsible, and her maintenance costs are predictable because issues are addressed proactively before they escalate. She has never faced a major lawsuit, a crippling city code violation, or a devastating tax penalty. She has even received unsolicited letters from neighbors, praising her property manager and mentioning how much they appreciate having a responsible owner on the block. This community goodwill has translated directly into word-of-mouth referrals for her vacant units, a sense of security for her assets, and a profound sense of pride in her investments. She has not just acquired properties; she has cultivated relationships and actively contributed to the stability and well-being of the communities she invested in.

Lena's success is not a fluke, nor is it a result of mere luck. It's a direct, undeniable consequence of her disciplined, ethical, and intelligent application of Strategy, Structure, and Support (S3). She didn't chase a dream; she built a sustainable, ethical business. She didn't buy blindly; she invested with eyes wide open, supported by a meticulously vetted network of trusted professionals. She didn't just seek a high ROI; she built a legacy of responsible ownership that profoundly benefited her, her tenants, and the communities she invested in. Her story is a powerful testament to the fact that the "right way" is not only possible but ultimately more profitable, infinitely more fulfilling, and truly sustainable.

Long-Term Vision: Patience, Consistency, and Community Engagement – The Pillars of Enduring Success

Lena's story highlights the core tenets of long-term success in inner-city real estate, principles that transcend mere financial metrics and delve into the very fabric of sustainable wealth creation. These are the operational and philosophical anchors that will keep your investment ship steady through any storm.

Firstly, **patience is a virtue, not a weakness: The Anti-Instant Gratification Mindset**. The "easy money" narrative, so prevalent in the miseducation, aggressively promotes instant gratification and quick, outsized returns. It creates an unhealthy expectation of rapid profits and encourages impulsive decisions. But real, sustainable wealth in real estate is built incrementally over time. It's about consistent, reliable cash flow, gradual, organic appreciation, and harnessing the immense, compounding power of equity buildup and reinvestment. Be prepared for the long haul. Understand that market cycles exist (and will fluctuate, sometimes dramatically). Don't panic at short-term fluctuations or minor setbacks. Your Strategy should be meticulously designed for years, even decades, not just for the next quarter or the next year. This long-term perspective allows you to weather economic downturns, make wise decisions that benefit both your portfolio and the community, and ultimately reap the compounding rewards of sustained growth and positive impact. It also frees you from the emotional rollercoaster of chasing every market swing. Patience is your strategic advantage against the short-sighted.

Secondly, **consistency in execution is the engine of reliability and trust**. This applies to every single aspect of your investment, from the micro-level details to the macro-level oversight. It means consistent property maintenance (proactive, not reactive, addressing issues before they become major problems), consistent tenant screening (no shortcuts, ever, regardless of how quickly you need to fill a vacancy), consistent financial reporting (meticulous, transparent, and on schedule), and consistent, proactive communication with your Support System. Inconsistent action inevitably leads to inconsistent results and, ultimately, escalating problems. Your Support System is absolutely key to maintaining this consistency, especially when you are operating from afar. They are your operational engine, ensuring that the day-to-day details are handled with the same diligence and precision you would apply if you were physically present. This unwavering consistency builds deep trust with tenants, contractors, and the community, creating a stable, predictable, and ultimately more profitable environment for your investment. It reduces surprises and fosters reliability.

Finally, **genuine community engagement is the unquantifiable, yet powerful, asset**. This goes far beyond just being a "good landlord" who collects rent and fixes leaks. It means actively understanding and respecting the local dynamics, supporting local businesses (where feasible, e.g., using local contractors or suppliers, patronizing neighborhood shops), and being aware of, and responsive to, community initiatives and concerns. Your property manager and local advisor should be your eyes and ears for this, actively fostering positive relationships on your behalf. When you contribute to the well-being of the community, even indirectly, your investment becomes more stable, more resilient, and more valuable. This isn't charity; it's profoundly smart business that builds a positive reputation, fosters a more secure environment for your assets, and can even lead to unique off-market opportunities through local connections. It's the ultimate form of long-term risk mitigation and value creation. A community that trusts you is a community that protects your investment, alerts you to problems, and provides a stable tenant base. This intangible goodwill is a powerful, compounding asset that no spreadsheet can fully capture.

Defining "Winning": Beyond the Numbers, Towards True Success

The miseducation taught you that winning was about owning the most doors, achieving the highest ROI percentages, or closing the fastest deals. These are merely metrics, often superficial, and not necessarily true definitions of sustainable success or personal fulfillment. Chasing these singular metrics without a holistic approach is how investors get burned, sacrificing long-term stability for short-term, often illusory, gains.

For the truly ready investor, winning is multi-faceted, encompassing both tangible and intangible returns, creating a holistic sense of accomplishment. Yes, it's undeniably about **sustainable financial stability**, meaning consistent, healthy cash flow and robust returns, but it's sustainable cash flow and realistic returns that allow you to sleep soundly at night. It's about building genuine equity through mortgage paydown and organic appreciation, protecting your initial capital, and generating predictable income that contributes to your overall financial freedom and long-term security. This means understanding the true costs, accounting for contingencies, and valuing long-term stability over short-term spikes. It's about building a financial engine that reliably serves your life goals.

This often leads to **profound peace of mind**, which is frequently the most valuable, yet unquantifiable, return on your investment. It's the profound sense of calm that comes from knowing that your investment is well-managed, legally protected, tax-optimized, and aligned with your personal values. It's the absence of constant anxiety and worry, the freedom from unexpected crises that consume your time and energy, and the quiet confidence that your assets are working for you, not against you. This peace of mind allows you to focus on other aspects of your life, rather than being perpetually stressed by your investments. It's the ultimate luxury.

For many, true winning extends far beyond purely financial gain to the **tangible impact and purpose** their investments have on people and places. This could mean providing safe, clean, and well-maintained affordable housing for families who desperately need it. It could mean contributing directly to the revitalization and stability of a neighborhood that has endured decades of neglect. It could mean creating local jobs for contractors and tradespeople, stimulating the local economy. These actions align your financial goals with a deeper sense of purpose, creating a legacy that is both profitable and profoundly meaningful. Your investment becomes a force for good, a testament to responsible capitalism.

Winning also involves **building an invaluable reputation**, becoming known as a fair, responsible, transparent, and professional investor. This reputation, built through consistent integrity and ethical practices, attracts better quality deals, more reliable tenants, and more trustworthy partners. It's a form of social capital that pays immense dividends, opening doors that remain closed to those who operate without principle. It's the ultimate long-term marketing strategy, creating a virtuous cycle of positive interactions and opportunities.

Finally, true success offers **scalability and sustainability** – the ability to confidently and strategically grow your portfolio, knowing that your robust Strategy, Structure, and Support systems can handle the expansion without compromising integrity, increasing undue risk, or leading to personal burnout. It means your investment model is repeatable, resilient, and built for the long haul, allowing you to achieve your financial goals without sacrificing your well-being or your peace of mind. It's about building an enduring enterprise, not just a collection of properties.

Winning, in this context, is about building a legacy—a lasting impact that extends far beyond your balance sheet. It's about creating something real, something that endures, and something you can be truly proud of, not just financially, but ethically, socially, and personally.

My Vision for the Future: Rebuilding What Was Stolen

I started this book by sharing my own painful journey into the "turnkey trap," the raw realization that even with the best intentions and deepest local knowledge, I could get lost in the very corruption and chaos I was fighting. That experience, and the countless stories of miseducated investors I've helped pull out of devastating situations, forged my unwavering commitment to this mission: to tell the truth, to expose the system, and to empower you to invest the right way. My vision is not just about individual success stories; it's about fundamentally shifting the paradigm of international real estate investment in the U.S. inner city.

My vision for the future of international real estate investing in the U.S. inner city is one where **transparency is the unquestionable standard, not an exception**. This means where information asymmetry is systematically dismantled, and investors have access to the full, unvarnished truth about properties, markets, and partners. It implies readily available, independently verified data, clear and comprehensive disclosures, and a culture where hiding information is met with severe consequences. It means leveraging technology to provide real-time, verifiable insights into property conditions and operational performance.

Furthermore, my vision is where **integrity is non-negotiable and actively rewarded**. Here, bad actors are swiftly exposed and held accountable, and legitimate, ethical professionals thrive and are celebrated. This creates an ecosystem built on deep trust, unwavering accountability, and mutual benefit, rather than exploitation. It means a market where doing things the right way is not just an option, but the most profitable, sustainable, and respected path. It means a community of investors and professionals who uphold the highest ethical standards.

A crucial part of this future is where **education is truly empowering and universally accessible**. Investors are not just sold dreams but are thoroughly and realistically educated in the fundamental principles of Strategy, Structure, and Support (S3), allowing them to make informed, confident, and proactive decisions. This education empowers them to discern genuine opportunity from deceptive hype, to ask the right questions, and to demand the right protections. It means providing practical, actionable knowledge that transforms novices into masters.

I envision a future where **investment creates true legacy and community prosperity**. This means international capital flows into communities not just for personal profit, but to genuinely improve housing stock, foster neighborhood stability, create local jobs, and contribute to the overall well-being and upliftment of residents. It implies a neighborhood's memory being filled with positive stories of responsible ownership, leading to a virtuous cycle of investment, community growth, and shared prosperity. This represents a shift from purely extractive investment to one that builds and contributes.

Ultimately, my vision is one where **you, the international investor, are a strategic player, not a vulnerable mark**. Equipped with the knowledge, the tools, and the meticulously vetted network to navigate this complex landscape successfully, you build wealth and purpose without fear of being exploited. You become an active participant, a leader in your own investment journey, capable of making informed decisions and demanding accountability from all parties. You are a force for positive change, a respected member of the community, and a master of your own financial destiny.

This is not a utopian dream. I have seen it happen. I have seen investors, like Lena, who have embraced this path and are building truly successful, sustainable portfolios while making a profound positive impact on the communities they touch. They are the living, breathing proof that investing the right way is not only possible but ultimately more profitable, infinitely more fulfilling, and truly sustainable in the long run. They are the pioneers of a new era of responsible international real estate investment, setting a new standard for others to follow.

Your Reset, Your Redemption, Your Rise: The Ultimate Call to Action

You have absorbed the truth. You understand the unseen game. You are no longer a target; you are a InvestorRedi™. The choice now is yours: Will you let this invaluable knowledge remain theoretical, a mere collection of insights, or will you activate it and transform your investment journey into a tangible reality?

Your journey to becoming a truly ready investor, one who builds legacy and not just ROI, begins with decisive action. Whether you choose to apply the principles of Strategy, Structure, and Support (S^3) independently, leveraging the tools and insights provided in this book, or through the comprehensive, hands-on guidance of the Investor

Readiness Certification™ program, the power is now firmly in your hands.

Remember, the block has memory. How you show up, how you invest, and the impact you make will resonate for years, even generations, to come. Choose to invest the right way. Choose to build with integrity. Choose to create a legacy that extends far beyond your balance sheet, enriching both your life and the communities you touch.

Let's rebuild what was stolen—starting with the truth and moving towards a legacy that truly lasts.

Final Reflection:

- What is the single most important takeaway you will apply from this book to your investment journey, starting today? How will this fundamentally change your approach to U.S. real estate and your decision-making process? Be specific.
- How will you define "winning" for your own real estate investments, beyond just financial metrics? What specific, non-financial impacts—on your family, your community, your peace of mind, your personal growth—do you genuinely want to achieve through your investments? Write these down as your personal mission statement.
- What is the very next concrete, actionable step you will take to move from learning to actively implementing the principles of Strategy, Structure, and Support (S3)? Be specific, set a realistic timeline (e.g., "Within 7 days, I will contact a U.S. attorney specializing in foreign investment to discuss LLC formation"), and commit to this crucial first step towards your Investor Readiness.

Hey there again,

As we close the pages of this book, I want to speak to you directly, from my heart to yours. My purpose in writing ***The Miseducation of the Foreign Real Estate Investor*** was never to sell you dreams—the market is already oversaturated with those. My purpose was, and remains, to tell you the unvarnished truth: the real game, the real risks that hide in plain sight, and the real, profound rewards that await those who choose to play it the right way.

I know this truth because I've lived it. I've walked the very streets I've described, seen the blight, and felt the pulse of communities often misunderstood. I've trusted the wrong people, swayed by promises that glittered but held no substance. I, too, thought that simply acquiring "one property" would magically change everything, only to learn that without the right **Strategy, Structure, and Support**, a property can become a burden, not a blessing. I've been the woman who almost let fear, frustration, and the sheer exhaustion of battling deception keep her out of the game entirely.

There was a time, I'll be honest, when I was so utterly frustrated, so completely disillusioned by the rampant scams, the shady operators, and the endless half-truths permeating the real estate world, that I took 18 months off. I was done. I was completely turned off by real estate, by the constant vigilance it demanded, by the betrayal I witnessed and experienced. My spirit was weary.

But in that period of quiet reflection, God kept laying it on my heart, a persistent whisper that grew into a clear command: "You can't just walk away. You have to do your part. You have a unique perspective, a hard-won truth. You must share it."

So, I came back—not just as an investor, but as an advocate, a truth-teller, and a relentless champion for every foreign investor who has been miseducated, misled, and left to figure it out alone. This book isn't just about deals or dollars. It's about redemption—the reclaiming of lost capital, lost peace of mind, and lost dreams. It's about empowering you to reclaim your future, to build something real and lasting, free from the shadows of deception.

This has become my unwavering mission—to stand in the gap, to illuminate the unseen game, and to bring real awareness and actionable solutions to this complex arena. My deepest desire is to show you how to play it smarter, safer, and stronger, with integrity and confidence. Because you, with your ambition and your willingness to invest, deserve nothing less than the truth and the tools to succeed.

So, here's my final word to you, as you embark on this next season of your investment journey:

Keep going. The path of the ready investor is not always easy, but it is profoundly rewarding. **Keep asking questions.** Never stop verifying, never stop learning, and never settle for vague answers. Your curiosity is your greatest protection. **Keep building smarter—not just bigger.** Prioritize the strength of your **Strategy, Structure, and Support** over the sheer number of properties. Quality over quantity, always. **Keep showing up.** Be present, be diligent, and hold your team accountable. Your consistent oversight is the engine of your success.

This isn't the end of your story—it's just the start of your next, most powerful season. You are now equipped. You are ready.

And most of all—keep remembering—you're not just buying properties. You're building a future. A future for yourself, your family, and, for the communities you touch.

I'm rooting for you. I'm standing with you. And I'm here to remind you—you're not alone.

Glossary of Terms: Foreign to Fluent

No more confusion—just clear, concise definitions of the key terms you'll encounter, transforming you from a miseducated novice to a fluent, confident investor.

- **1031 Exchange:** A method under U.S. tax law that allows investors to defer capital gains taxes when selling one investment property and reinvesting the proceeds into another "like-kind" property. Requires strict adherence to IRS rules and timelines.
- **After Repair Value (ARV):** The estimated value of a property after all necessary repairs and renovations have been completed. Crucial for fix-and-flip strategies.
- **Appreciation:** The increase in a property's value over time.
- **Asset Protection:** Strategies (like forming an LLC) used to shield personal assets from liabilities arising from business activities.
- **Capital Expenditure (CapEx):** Significant, infrequent expenses for major repairs or improvements that extend the life of a property (e.g., new roof, HVAC, foundation repair). Distinct from routine maintenance.
- **Capitalization Rate (Cap Rate):** A measure of a property's profitability, calculated as Net Operating Income (NOI) divided by the property's purchase price. Used to compare investment properties.
- **Cash Flow:** The net income generated by a property after all operating expenses and debt service (mortgage payments) are paid. Positive cash flow means money in your pocket.
- **Cash-on-Cash Return (CoC):** A measure of the annual pre-tax cash flow generated by a property, divided by the total cash invested (down payment, closing costs, initial rehab). Expressed as a percentage.
- **Certificate of Occupancy (CO):** A document issued by a local government agency certifying that a building complies with

applicable building codes and other laws and is safe for occupancy. Essential for legal renting.

- **Code Violation:** A breach of local building, housing, or zoning ordinances, often resulting in fines or mandatory repairs.
- **Condemnation:** A legal declaration by a government authority that a property is unsafe or unfit for human habitation, often leading to demolition or mandatory extensive repairs.
- **Due Diligence:** The process of conducting thorough research and investigation of a property and deal before committing to a purchase, to identify all potential risks and verify all information.
- **Due-on-Sale Clause:** A mortgage clause that requires the borrower to repay the entire loan balance upon the sale or transfer of the property.
- **Employer Identification Number (EIN):** A unique nine-digit tax identification number assigned by the IRS to businesses operating in the U.S.
- **FIRPTA (Foreign Investment in Real Property Tax Act):** A U.S. tax law that requires buyers to withhold 15% of the gross sales price when a foreign person sells U.S. real property and remit it to the IRS.
- **Hard Money Loan:** A short-term, high-interest loan typically used by real estate investors for flips or properties that don't qualify for traditional financing.
- **Limited Liability Company (LLC):** A popular U.S. business entity that provides personal liability protection for its owners, separating personal assets from business debts and lawsuits.
- **Lien:** A legal claim against a property, typically for a debt owed (e.g., tax lien, mechanic's lien for unpaid contractor work).
- **Micro-Market:** A specific, small geographical area (e.g., a few blocks or a specific neighborhood) within a larger city, characterized by its own unique demographics, property values, and market dynamics.

- **Net Operating Income (NOI):** A property's income after all operating expenses have been deducted, but before accounting for mortgage payments or income taxes.
- **Pro Forma:** A financial projection or forecast for a property's income and expenses, often provided by sellers to illustrate potential returns. Should always be independently verified and adjusted.
- **Property Management Agreement (PMA):** A legally binding contract between a property owner and a property management company, outlining roles, responsibilities, fees, and terms.
- **Section 8 Housing:** A federal program that provides housing assistance to low-income families, the elderly, and people with disabilities, often guaranteeing a portion of the rent payment from the government.
- **Scope of Work (SOW):** A detailed document outlining all tasks, materials, and specifications for a renovation or repair project.
- **Title Insurance:** An insurance policy that protects the buyer and/or lender against financial loss due to defects in the title to a property.
- **Turnkey Property:** A property advertised as "ready to rent" or "renovated and tenant-occupied," implying minimal effort for the investor. Often a term used by unscrupulous sellers to disguise problems.
- **Vacancy Rate:** The percentage of time a rental property is unoccupied. A key factor in financial projections.

Tools, Sites & Software

Disclaimer: Use at your own risk.

Empower Your Investment Journey: Essential Tools & Resources

Navigating the U.S. real estate market, particularly as a foreign investor, requires meticulous due diligence, streamlined operations, and a robust support system. To truly succeed, you need the right tools at your fingertips.

Your Essential Investment Workbook

Start your comprehensive due diligence today! Download our **Foreign Investor Due Diligence Workbook** directly from InvestorRedi.com to gain critical insights and frameworks for evaluating potential investments.

Inside, you'll discover actionable frameworks and critical tools, including:

- **Foreign Investor Due Diligence Checklist:** Navigate the specific complexities unique to international real estate investment.
- **Team Vetting Script Templates:** Build your reliable U.S. support system with confidence and clarity.
- **Deal Evaluation Worksheet:** Systematically assess potential investments to maximize your profitability.
- **Glossary of U.S. Real Estate Terms:** Demystify industry jargon and speak the language of the American market.

Don't leave your investment to chance. Download your complete workbook now:

InvestorRedi.com/workbook

Leverage these powerful resources to empower your due diligence, streamline your operations, and stay informed every step of the way. Remember: tools are only as good as the hand that wields them, and they should always be used in conjunction with your trusted Support System.

Key Resources for Every Stage of Your Investment:

Here's a curated list of digital tools and essential practices to support your U.S. real estate ventures:

For Property & Market Comps (Research & Valuation):

- **Rentometer.com:** Quickly provides estimated market rent for a specific address based on recent rentals in the area. Great for initial rent comparisons.
- **Zillow.com / Redfin.com / Realtor.com:** Excellent for researching property values, recent sales comparables, active listings, and rental listings. Use their "Sold" filters to see actual transaction prices.
- **City/County Assessor Websites:** Search by address for public property tax records, assessed values, and ownership history. These public records are invaluable for verification.
- **Local MLS (Multiple Listing Service):** Your local real estate agent will have access to the most comprehensive and up-to-date sales and rental data. This is your primary source for accurate comparables.

For Property Management & Accounting (Operations & Structure):

- **Buildium.com / AppFolio.com / Propertyware.com:** Industry-leading property management software platforms. They handle rent collection, expense tracking, tenant communication, maintenance requests, and comprehensive financial reporting. Your property manager will likely utilize one of these, and you should ensure you have owner access.
- **QuickBooks Online / Xero:** Cloud-based accounting software that allows you to efficiently manage your business finances, track income and expenses, and generate professional financial reports. Essential for maintaining clean books for your U.S. entity.

For Communication & Documentation (Support & Structure):

- **Google Drive / Dropbox / Microsoft OneDrive:** Robust cloud-based storage solutions for securely organizing and sharing all your property documents (leases, inspection reports, invoices, photos, videos) with your team. Ensure you establish clear, intuitive folder structures.
- **Notion.so / Asana / Trello:** Powerful project management and collaboration tools that can be utilized to efficiently track rehabilitation projects, manage maintenance requests, and maintain clear communication logs with your entire team.
- **WhatsApp / Email:** While useful for quick communication and general updates, always ensure all critical decisions and documentation are formally recorded and saved in a more permanent and organized system (e.g., email threads saved, key decisions summarized and stored in a shared document).

Pro Tip: Always Call the City Directly!

For any property you're serious about, have your local Support System (or your attorney) directly call the city's building department, code enforcement, and housing court for that specific address. This direct verification step often reveals critical information that Google won't, the seller might not disclose, and a quick online search could easily miss. This is often the most powerful due diligence step you can take.

Key questions to ask your Support System to verify:

- Are there any open code violations currently associated with the property?
- What is the permit history for any past renovations or construction?
- What is the current rental registration status and Certificate of Occupancy?
- Are there any pending legal actions or condemnation orders against the property?

Shemika Jackson, also known as Meek the House Geek, is not just a real estate investor—she's a mission-driven advocate and a relentless truth-teller for foreign investors who've been left in the dark for far too long. A serial entrepreneur at heart, Shemika has built multiple successful businesses from the ground up, blending raw grit, invaluable real-world experience, and an unwavering commitment to helping others win.

Known for her candid, no-nonsense approach and her ability to cut through the industry hype, Shemika has spent years navigating the complex and often treacherous world of U.S. real estate. She has walked the streets, seen the scams, and experienced firsthand the devastating consequences of miseducation, both as an active investor and as a licensed real estate agent. She is the founder of InvestorRedi™, a groundbreaking, premium program meticulously designed to empower international buyers, transforming them into credible, strategically structured, and fully equipped investors poised to thrive in the American property market. Her work isn't just about helping people buy houses—it's about giving them the comprehensive blueprint to build lasting legacies and secure their financial futures.

Shemika's real estate journey is deeply personal and rooted in authenticity. She grew up in the inner city of Cleveland, in the very neighborhoods that foreign investors often see as "cheap buys" but profoundly misunderstand beyond the price tag. She's witnessed firsthand how misinformation, predatory practices, and shady deals can devastate families and communities—and she's made it her life's mission to fight back against this systemic miseducation.

For Shemika, real estate isn't just business—it's ministry. She believes every investor, regardless of their origin, deserves the unvarnished truth, and every neighborhood deserves genuine stewardship and responsible ownership. Her passion is to bridge the gap between aspiration and reality, empowering investors to make a positive impact while achieving their financial goals.

Beyond the business, Shemika is a devoted mom of four, a woman of profound faith, and someone who has learned the immense power of resilience, both in the challenging world of real estate and in the journey of life itself. When she's not turning broken houses into opportunity or turning clients into confident, ready investors, you'll find her sharing real talk, behind-the-scenes insights, and empowering messages on social media as @MeekTheHouseGeek.

www.ingramcontent.com/pod-product-compliance
Lightning Source LLC
La Vergne TN
LVHW102227300926
849160LV00005B/58
* 9 7 9 8 9 9 9 1 0 8 7 7 7 *